The Future of the American Family

An Unprecedented Crisis

by

Dr. Jerry Cammarata

E&R

PUBLISHERS OF O.G AUTHOR GENIUSES

Published by E&R Publishers
New York, NY, USA

An imprint of MillsoCo Publishing, USA
www.EandR.pub

ISBN: 9798990521759 Hardcover
ISBN: 9798990521766 Paperback
ISBN: 9798990521773 Ebook
Library of Congress Control Number: 2024944665

MISSION

This book gives the reasons why the family has been in decline for generations. The solution is clear, and here it is in a nutshell: To make the American Family the gold standard for raising children, having a home-work balanced life, and the best-educated society. Each is explained and is unconditional if we are to succeed as the America we claim to be or aspire to.

1. Create a Secretary of the Family - Cabinet Position
2. Commence a White House Conference on Families
3. A National Paid Family Leave Policy (No talk, action—finally)
4. Establish the National Education Contract (NEC)—local Colleges, high schools, elementary schools, Pre-K schools, and special education schools, must all participate in the Pre-K to 16 education of every student, all as a part of the reconfiguration of the Federal Department of Education. A local education success initiative.
5. Incentivize corporate America to redesign and restructure the workplace to honor the family worker.

DEDICATION

To the family. It has become my lifelong dedication.

The term "A good family" means different things to different people. To me, a good family can give you the nourishment to metabolize the world around you, understand the value and purpose of the human experience, and give you a healthy perspective on your life and the future.

CONTENTS

ENDORSEMENTS

"Government needs to listen to what Dr. Cammarata is saying about the future of the American family. Government and business must see the family as the center of our culture which will be the future success of our nation. Working toward a national family leave policy is another moment in our civil rights journey but the idea of a secretary of the family and a reestablishment of a White House Conference on Families is the type of thinking we need for extraordinary and permanent change for the better. Family first is vital to the restoration of civil rights in our nation and the restoration of the family to greatness. Jerry gets it."

—David A. Paterson, 55th Governor of New York

"The impact Dr. Jerry Cammarata has had on the Parental Leave issue over the last 50 years has been profound. Yes, our American Family is threatened and must be put on a road to recovery. Dr. Cammarata provides a clear and thoughtful approach to the rise again of the American Family."

—Steve Aiello - listing his BOE and white house credentials

"As a publisher reaching hundreds of thousands of readers every week, I know how important it is to reach the public with important information to improve lives. Dr. Cammarata's Book on the future of the American Family is that important information which gives us solutions which could change the way we look at the family forever."

—Victoria Schneps—President and Co—Schneps Media

They tell a story of a man who won the first Paternity Leave in the United States 50 years ago. Dr. Jerry Cammarata, is that man who today speaks to the present landscape of the family in America and its decline. He captures the essence of the distress, the forces which have failed the american family to thrive. This is a must read for all parents, corporate CEOs, and particularly our current administration which can change the way families will be treated in the future. This book can avert a national family crisis."

—Jerilyn Kronen, PhD—Psychologist in Family Practice

"Our american family life is facing so many challenges. Dr. Jerry Cammarata's book, The Future of the American Family, addresses key pillars of family life which require our immediate attention moving forward. This book will surely stimulate discussions and actions on the federal and municipal levels. We must all play a strategic role in redefining family policies and Practices."

—Joseph DeStefano—Mayor of the City of Middletown, New York

"Dr. Jerry Cammarata is extraordinarily creative and intelligent. He demonstrates great wisdom and a first-rate mind in his critical and comprehensive analysis of the family as the foundation of our national prosperity. This book is brilliant with respect to an activist roadmap by directly challenging our thought processes with recommendations for fundamental change towards new governmental constructs to enhance our quality of life. It is exciting, fun, and revolutionary!"

—Dr. John J. McGrath—CEO and President of Empire Education Corporation and Mildred Elley College

"I am in a business where the most important factor is 'engagement' of the audience. Are they forward in their chairs and listening deeply? Do I have their primary focused attention? Well, Dr. Jerry Cammarata had mine. His book, *The Future of the American Family—An Unprecedented Crisis*, is written so deeply, and its metaphors are so universal that his insights engage us all. He sounds a justified alarm about the American family and how that steadfastness of keeping the family together is cast against a capitalist society that loves 'new.' As divorce rates hit their highest numbers, the family remains the greatest glue and the greatest challenge in our society."
—Tovah Feldshuh, Award-winning actress, playwright, producer, and author

"Can the family unit survive and prosper? In The Future of the American Family, Dr. Jerry Cammarata not only poses that fundamental question, but he also profoundly offers his thesis on the challenges facing today's families, the guardrails to maintaining familial durability, and a prescription for family perseverance and peace."
—David Laurell, Former Mayor, City of Burbank, California

ACKNOWLEDGMENTS

There are so many to thank and acknowledge that I've decided instead to leave it up to you. Please scan the QR code below and sign my guest book. Leave a message about our interaction, why you have this book, and what it means to you, and my list of acknowledgments will live on as we all travel journeys that will have bumps in the road but will be hopeful, we will get to Disney World before the admissions fee gets so high that families will be prohibited to get in.

PROLOGUE

Who knew that at age four putting a 100-piece jigsaw puzzle together would compare in difficulty and complexity to negotiating a full life? Just emptying the box of all the pieces onto the table was enough pressure alone. The cover of the box indicates that there is a world order, a master plan that can be achieved, but how? Where do you start? Which piece do I pick up first? Of course, retrospectively, the corners are a great place to begin. But at four, who knew?

I recall hearing my mom remind me that Aunt Frances gave me the puzzle for my fourth birthday. It was supposedly not just a gift but part of a thought process she must have had to think the puzzle would be good for me. How can a puzzle be good for me? It wasn't food, I couldn't wear it. But my mom said to me, "Isn't this a beautiful gift? Something that will keep you busy and help you to think."

Well, I had an idea about the process of putting the puzzle together, but every time I reached a moment of indecision, I needed help, and the puzzle project became a nightmare for my mom because I would yell out to her constantly for help! Help! Help!

Today, it's 77 years later, and that puzzle is still on my mind. Heck, in retrospect, my whole life has been that puzzle; your whole life has been either that puzzle or some sort of project activity. That puzzle was the project of life skills building, which had the potential to make you or break you at the age of four.

It is this magic circle of influences we were born into, and at whatever age you want to tell your story, you just have to reflect upon what you were given. There's not much choice when you are just four; the food is put in front of you, and you just have to eat.

This story has been going on in humans' lives, and, for those of you who have had the opportunity to read my book, *The Fun Book of Fatherhood*, it is no less important in the lives of animal parents and children.

It is the story of having something, figuring out what to do with it, getting help to understand it, learning operational skills along the way, relying less upon others for help in completing the task while, at other times, discovering some really nifty ways of doing it your own way—kind of an invention you discovered—and then for the world to open up before you, one day at a time, one learning experience at a time. With all that help, encouragement, positivity, and nurturing from your parents—not to mention the hugs—you're finally on your way to conquering the world and using your puzzle skills to get on with your life.

So, where did the puzzle go wrong? Why aren't there more puzzle stories out there? Are puzzles so hard to find? Are puzzles no longer given as gifts? Do parents have no time to spend with their children to lessen the burdensome task of putting a puzzle together? Do you think there has been some news alert—coming from a prominent child psychologist perhaps—suggesting that giving puzzles to children at an early age could tax their motivation to learn and diminish their intellectual growth pattern? Or do you think they are just not making lots of puzzles today because the digital age is taking over the puzzle world? Maybe, with all this urban density concentration, we just don't have homes big enough to keep puzzles around.

What do you think as you reflect back on your young days? What was your puzzle experience? What was that toy you received that opened your mind to the possibility of doing something that had a beginning, middle, and end to the project? One that you completed, and you felt good because you had conquered, you had achieved. It's all about the puzzle. Wherever we are today, it was because of that puzzle and all the formative puzzle-like situations that ensued.

One friend of mine had a father who simply threw him into the deep end of the swimming pool to teach him to swim. Not the metaphorical pool, but an actual swimming pool. Now, I'm not recommending that this is good parenting by any means, but the fact is, this particular person did become an excellent swimmer and developed extraordinary survival skills that stood him in good stead for success after success.

Had it been a different child, it could have been a very different outcome, but my point is, that experience was dramatic to him—perhaps because his mother reminded him of it for many years to come because she was horrified that his father would do such a thing—but he wore it like a badge of honor because to him, he had conquered something through that experience and it had made him stronger. Then, of course, he adopted a similar approach to fathering, much to the chagrin of his wife, but this pattern exists in every culture. A big, life-altering experience. In some cultures, to become a man, for example, you must go out hunting by yourself overnight and bring back a slain grizzly bear the next day. I'm glad I wasn't in that village. Little things and big things can influence us in profound ways.

This book is similar to that puzzle. It is the shuffle of one shape to another early in life, the discovery process that forms the building blocks of our learning, and the social arena in which we find ourselves that creates the brushstrokes for the painting of our life, our puzzle. Are all the pieces still there? Are there any pieces missing? Are there any regrets or thoughts that perhaps a different puzzle picture might have been nicer or easier?

You have choices in the exercise of reading this book. As you draw conclusions from reflections on your life experiences, you can lament, regret, build new ideas to share, or simply accept what was and leave it at that. You could put your whole life before you and think about what changes in direction you could have made that would have transformed you into a "better" person. You could take who you are now and have boundless gratitude for how you have turned out and how far you have come. Either way, for the rest of your life, you will work on puzzles. Perhaps you will work on them with others in the hope they may have a better tomorrow in their life.

Another of my friends is a wonderful mother, and her children are models of good character, happiness, and success. However, when she reflects on her child-raising, there are so many things she would change if she had the chance to do it again. That being said, those children may have received character-building lessons and traits because of her self-perceived mistakes as a mother. It depends on the child, the "village," the opportunities, and the sheer luck of it all in some cases. We usually parent how we were parented, but as time goes on, some break out of that mold, learn more about the psychology of how children are affected by certain behaviors, and change how they do things, thereby breaking the chain of child-raising techniques and behaviors. When people talk about generational trauma, this is the root cause. At a cellular level, trauma can be embedded and continue through generations.

The journey we will take together is one of enlightenment, and I sincerely hope that with all the puzzles gone wrong in the great society we call America, we can change—or else we'll see the American family puzzle end up in a crisis, with missing pieces. Our puzzles of life can be enriching and so powerful that every piece of daily living builds each child and each parent in

America to be outstanding. Those small puzzles in our early lives with parents and other support groups around us can be magnified beyond our wildest imagination to become a national puzzle of international prominence.

This is our book and our journey together. We will examine our American family and see what has been and what is happening to it and where the "corruption," or deviation from the path has taken place. It is in places we would never have imagined. It is in the corners of our lives that we have been celebrating for years, if not for decades, if not for centuries; yet, it has been toxic and must change.

Let the puzzle box be opened, pour the pieces out, and I can't wait to meet you at the epilogue to examine our completed puzzle together.

1. DEFCON 1

THE ALARM CAN NEVER BE LOUDER THAN NOW!

"The strength of a nation derives from the integrity of the home."
—Confucius

What you are about to read cannot be described as important; it is a DEFCON 1, three-alarm warning previsioning the demise of the American family the way that we know it. It is not what might happen, it is what has already happened. To put it into perspective, compared to climate change warning signs, imagine it is 125 degrees, the food chain has begun breaking down, lower Manhattan is under water due to rising sea level, and half the world is on fire. Like a frog in boiling water, we are not even aware that we're already cooked. This book will explore how we got here and where we will be if we stay on this trajectory.

Who are we as a country if not a parade of families proud of who we are and where we have come from? Our red, white, and blue pride, our diversity under one flag, how could this mosaic of the American family have become so off track, misused, and moving toward extinction? A cacophony of events—purposefully and unwittingly—has pushed the American family to the cliff. We await its fall in a sea of ignorance—a **CRISIS** that could have been avoided! A crisis caused by us, we should have seen it coming, we continually fed the crisis fire with rules, law, and policy. We watched it burn and now we can't figure out how to put the fire out. This book can put the family crisis fire out!

In this unprecedented jeopardy, what threatens the American family's survival is profound and ubiquitous. These threats surround us and launch slow but endless attacks from every perceivable and imperceivable angle. They erode what remains of our most precious asset; the center of our reason for being—the family. We have used our societal institutions, not to serve the family but—selfishly—for other than the pure intentions of purpose. Just look at the manner in which we execute our laws, policies, and attitudes.

Our perception of the quintessential American family, the one that is reflected in the old TV sitcoms that contain a mother, a father, two children—usually a boy and a girl—makes up about only 8% of American families today but the path of diversity of the family is not the problem either, in fact, diversity makes us ever-stronger through solid executive immigration policies. The real threats are the quiet, unseen ones. The ones that sneak in at night in the dark, while we snuggle down in presumed safety and comfort. Now, finally, we're waking up and realizing the mess we are in.

- The idea of the nuclear family—the concept of the isolated nucleus—evolved over time. It began in Europe and found its way to America while in our formative years. The breakdown of "The Village"—the community that surrounded our families that helped raise them with the wisdom of the hive mind—the elders, the diversity of experience, age, and abilities: this is where the threat first began.
- The September 11, 2001, terrorist attacks had profound and far-reaching effects on American families, impacting them in several significant ways. Thousands of families lost loved ones in the attacks, leading to widespread grief and trauma. The sudden and violent nature of the event made the mourning process particularly difficult. The attacks also instilled a sense of vulnerability and fear in many American families. Concerns about future terrorist attacks, personal safety, and national security became more pronounced.

  Families—especially those directly affected or living in New York and Washington, D.C.—experienced post-traumatic stress disorder. This included not just survivors but also first responders and witnesses whose families had to support them through their recovery.

  For some, however, the attacks led to a renewed emphasis on family, with individuals prioritizing relationships and spending more time with loved ones, recognizing the fragility of life.

  In contrast, the stress and anxiety resulting from the attacks led to strained relationships in some families, with increased rates of divorce and familial discord reported in the years following 9/11.

  The economic downturn following 9/11, particularly in industries like travel, tourism, and insurance, led to job losses and financial difficulties for many families. The uncertainty of the economy added additional stress to family life.

Families of those who worked in the World Trade Center or Pentagon, as well as those living nearby, faced displacement. Some were forced to relocate due to the destruction of homes and workplaces.

Children, in particular, were affected by the fear and confusion surrounding the attacks. Many were exposed to distressing images and news coverage, leading to anxiety and questions about safety and the world around them.

The attacks fostered a surge in patriotism and a collective sense of national identity. Families across the country engaged in activities that promoted unity, such as flying American flags and participating in community service. This patriotism may have also contributed to a significant increase in military enlistment. This led to extended deployments for military families, resulting in long periods of separation, anxiety, and the challenges associated with reintegration after service. Ultimately though, the patriotism which glowed from coast to coast was short lived.

The subsequent wars in Afghanistan and Iraq created a new generation of Gold Star families—a modern reference that comes from the Service Flag—who lost loved ones in military service. These families faced unique grief and challenges, including public recognition and the burden of loss.

Heightened security measures, particularly in airports, became a new norm for American families. The experience of traveling changed drastically, with longer wait times and increased scrutiny affecting the ease and spontaneity of family vacations and visits.

The implementation of the USA PATRIOT Act and other security measures raised concerns about privacy and civil liberties, with some families feeling the effects of increased government surveillance and changes in the legal landscape.

Overall, the 9/11 attacks reshaped the American family in both tangible and intangible ways. The emotional, economic, and social impacts of the event continued to resonate for years, influencing family dynamics, cultural norms, and the overall sense of security within American society. Everything chips away at our precious family structures and we're just not paying attention to the erosion.

- Social media is a natural evolution. As water finds its own path, people seek and find their village and while the nuclear family is isolated by nature, the inhabitants become vulnerable. Children will naturally seek what they feel is missing whether it be acceptance, attention, or like-mindedness. In the village, there was always somebody who saw potential in someone and could mentor them. They saw what others did not see because of the diversity of the wider family and that knowledge was shared within the safe confines of the village. With the absence of the village, we seek what is inherently missing and in this borderless, insecure portal direct into our children's lives. This secret gateway that allows unprecedented influence over our children.

- Artificial intelligence, while still nascent, has provided the fastest sweeping change in our lives in history. My generation were born at a time that allowed us to experience the birth and evolution of rock and roll, stereo music, eight tracks, cassettes, CDs, MP3s, and streaming—and that's just music. Television, color television, VCRs, TIVO, on-demand streaming. Helicopters, microwaves, polaroids, and atomic weapons. Mobile phones, scanning, faxing, the internet, fingerprinting, artificial hearts, DNA… It's not an exhaustive list but it's exhausting thinking about the breakneck speed of change over only one lifetime. Now we have AI, which promises to deliver an acceleration of technological change that will dwarf the arc of my entire generation.
- The Pandemic had a profound effect on the nature of family as people, faced with a new world of isolation, chose those to call family and built synthetic new family ties—again, water finding its own path.
- Education has changed in nature and since the introduction of student loans that burden children for entire chunks of their lives just to get a mediocre (in many cases) credentialing so that they can move into a world that they used to naturally progress to. The modern American family's focus on getting their children through college is an all-encompassing and mostly destructive practice. In the book *The End of College* by Kevin Carey, the author reveals that 60% of people do not come out of college any smarter or more knowledgeable whatsoever. It is only the 40% who are naturally suited to this style of learning that benefit from the practice. The rest all just get debt and lose years of their lives that could have been spent out in the world creating something for themselves.

But it's not social media, AI, or the lack of responsible education alone that is eroding the family; it is the complete lack of focus on the family. The abandonment of family care over the everyday busy-work of government. As politicians do battle to control the world, they do not do battle for the family. The American family is starving for meaningful attention, for its place on the national stage, yet it can't take a bow these days.

We can survive practically any administration because there is a constant scuffle for balance. A pendulum that swings back and forth due to the opposing forces pushing back on each other. Like iron sharpening iron, one party holds the other to account and vice versa but the poor old family is not even in the conversation. It just gets dragged along like a plastic bag behind a truck in this selfish battle for control.

We'd rather talk about taxable income rates, inflation, procedure, defense, and almost anything rather than the central issue of protecting families and giving them the resources to thrive in a new and strange landscape. It's a gigantic puzzle that nobody is trying to solve and if we don't do anything and stay on the current trajectory, in the next 20–30 years the American family will be unrecognizable and non-salvageable for all intents and purposes. Now let's explore that puzzle through the eyes of the family.

The Fragile Foundation: Education and America's Place in the World

Imagine Kodak, a company that once dominated global photography, employing 160,000 people and responsible for 85% of the world's photos. In 1997, it seemed untouchable, but the rise of mobile cameras made Kodak obsolete. Eventually, the company declared bankruptcy, leaving its workforce behind. Kodak wasn't alone. Icons like Nokia, Compaq, BlackBerry, Toys "R" Us, Blockbuster, Borders, Studebaker, Polaroid, Palm, MySpace, Napster, Pan Am, and AltaVista have disappeared, not due to poor quality but because they failed to adapt. Brands such as Sears and Yahoo are hanging on by a thread, with Yahoo's ubiquity diminished immeasurably and the once thousands of Sears stores is down to nine with two more closing at the time of this writing.

Many of these companies overestimated their brand power, underestimated emerging technologies and changing consumer behavior, and failed to pivot their business models in time. Their stories serve as cautionary tales about the importance of constant innovation and agility in the face of a rapidly changing marketplace.

Now, think of today's titans. Uber is the largest taxi service in the world, yet it owns no cars. Airbnb, the world's largest accommodation provider, doesn't own a single property for rent. These companies exemplify how innovation and adaptation are essential in a rapidly changing world.

We are on the brink of a Fourth Industrial Revolution, where automation, artificial intelligence, and digitalization are poised to redefine industries. Legal and medical AI outperforms human lawyers and doctors in specific tasks, signaling a seismic shift in professions. Cars, once symbols of personal freedom, will become driverless utilities, reducing traffic accidents, cutting insurance needs, and shrinking the workforce behind traditional auto industries.

For America, the implications are profound. If our education system doesn't evolve, the workforce will be unprepared for this future. Current predictions suggest 70–90% of today's jobs could vanish within a decade. Those who adapt, the experts, will thrive. The rest may well be left behind.

This transformation doesn't stop at employment. Financial systems, transportation, and even societal norms are shifting. Cash gave way to credit cards, and now mobile wallets dominate. Shopping has moved online, shrinking physical retail. Even seemingly secure roles like traffic officers and parking attendants could disappear as automation and smart systems take over.

The lesson is clear: adapt or risk irrelevance. And yet, America's education system—designed for the needs of the 20th century—is failing to prepare future generations for the 21st. If we don't prioritize innovation in learning, critical thinking, and adaptability, the nation risks losing its position as the global leader and custodian of democracy.

In a world where those who fail to change are left behind, the American family faces an urgent challenge: how do we equip the next generation to lead, innovate, and preserve the values that made the United States a beacon of hope? The answer begins with education—its transformation will determine whether we remain the architects of the future or spectators to our decline.

The United States is not even in the top 10 countries with the longest life expectancy. We are not in the top 10 (not even on the list) for universal health care. Yes, we are in the top 10 of having one of the world's great landmarks—the Statue of Liberty—but does it symbolize everything the American family needs, deserves, and should be getting? We are low on the scale for child mortality, 55th on maternal health care, education… We are so low on so many scales yet we profess to be the best country in the world. Why is that! Self-preservation?

Imagine if the family was the gold standard. We would be making sure that every decision made in life was focused on the family being the best and getting the best.

The only state that grew in population significantly in 2023 was Texas. California's population shrank by 0.19%, losing 75,423 people due to high costs and housing availability. West Virginia declined by 0.22% due to economic issues and younger residents leaving. Illinois declined by 0.26% in 2023, losing 32,8726. Louisiana lost 0.31% or 14,274 people due to natural disasters and economic challenges, but the biggest loser of all was New York. NYC's population was estimated at 8.26 million as of July 1, 2023, a decrease of 78,000 since July 1, 2022, and of 546,000 since the April 1, 2020, Census enumeration of 8.80 million. Population losses have attenuated each year between 2020 and 2023, with the bulk of estimated losses occurring early in the pandemic.

In 2023, states like New York, California, Illinois, West Virginia, and Louisiana experienced population declines due to residents relocating to other regions. The primary destinations for these individuals have been states in the South and West, notably Florida, Texas, Georgia, South Carolina, and Tennessee. These states have attracted new residents due to factors such as lower living costs, favorable tax policies, and warmer climates.

For instance, Florida's population reached a record high of over 23 million, with the state adding between 350,000 and 375,000 new residents annually over the past decade. Similarly, Texas led the nation in population growth between July 2022 and July 2023, adding nearly half a million new residents.

This migration trend reflects a broader pattern of individuals moving from high-cost states to regions offering more affordable living conditions and perceived better quality of life. The influx of new residents into these southern states has contributed significantly to their population growth in recent years.

This is a clear indication that people are trying to fight against the cost of living overtaking the income and one of the most important factors in the outcome of the 2024 election. But moving won't solve this problem long term. We must realign or the cost of living will catch up wherever we are.

2. THE 2024 ELECTION AND THE FAMILY

"Change is the law of life. And those who look only to the past or present are certain to miss the future."
—John F. Kennedy

Florida. November 2024

Finally, the hot water is back on, and folks can take a shower after 3 days of there being no electricity in the neighborhood. It's funny what a hurricane can do. It can upturn your life and make you appreciate what you need, what you want, and, quite frankly, what you have worked so hard for all your life. How dare Mother Nature take it away. After all, with many of us, life is about me! We may not Admit it—we were taught about feeding the hungry and doing unto others as they would do unto you—but it really is about "me!"

Now, let's explore another kind of hurricane. For many, a political hurricane just occurred, and rather than it being a cleansing wind, a new beginning with purifying rain and the ultimate ray of hope in the form of clouds parting and the sun emerging, for many, it wasn't that at all. We have a division in our beautiful country like nothing we have seen before. For those whose candidate did not make it, the outcome seems unimaginable, but let's take a look at the simple why. It's really not overly complicated. To many Americans, prosperity is often measured by a job and how much it pays. But there's something far more difficult to quantify that's missing from that simplistic picture. White men working without a college degree in 1980 made more money than the average American worker does today. As inflation has quietly eroded the quality of life for workers for the last 40 years, with income remaining relatively flat, we have a situation resembling a frog slowly boiling in water. He doesn't know he's boiling until it's so hot he can't get out.

Also, since 1980, white men without a degree have been surpassed in income by college-educated women. What this means is that relative standing has changed—how people fare compared to others. As we moved away from manufacturing and toward knowledge work, jobs that helped build the nation, like the machinists and metalworkers who were mostly white men without college degrees, have all but disappeared. In one's lifetime, experiencing a shrinking share while newer kinds of work—like financial analysis and software development—come to pay much more, it is easy for resentment to build. The economy has somewhat devalued the work and skills of some Americans while delivering mounting rewards to others. Reordering the status of workers increasingly shapes the country's politics. Your sense of worth is bound to diminish if, in relative terms, your income is declining. It may not be something that we monitor, but over time, like the boiling frog, they feel them.

College-educated men have been at the top of the food chain consistently, while women without a degree have long remained at the bottom. While these numbers have not significantly changed, workers in coastal states have seen the highest growth, while steep declines have been concentrated in parts of the Midwest, and this was certainly reflected in voting in November 2024. A factory foreman without a college degree in 1980 was a great American job. Supervisory roles made more than average workers four decades ago, even more than computer programmers. Today, however, those computer programmers make much more and are far higher in the economic ranks. In fact, nurses and dental hygienists make more than factory supervisors.

Largest gains	Largest losses
1. Computer programmers	1. Construction supervisors
2. Financial specialists	2. Mining supervisors
3. Securities, commodities, and financial services sales	3. Butchers and meat processors
	4. Transportation supervisors
4. Other sales workers	5. Radio and telecom workers
5. Pharmacists	6. Brick masons
6. Doctors and surgeons	7. Truck and tractor drivers
7. Lawyers and judges	8. Shipping clerks
8. Bank and financial clerks	9. Postal clerks
9. Registered nurses	10. Metal and plastic workers
10. Dentists	11. Stock clerks and order fillers

These trends go a long way to explaining the recent election results. Some are calling it the testosterone election. Many men are stuck: isolated, despairing, unproductive, prone to obesity, drug addiction, and suicide, and susceptible to misogyny, conspiracy theories, and radicalization. They make inadequate mates, employees, and citizens. Young men in America are grappling with the challenges of underemployment and a lack of social engagement. Rising tuition fees have created financial barriers for students of all genders, but since 2011, college enrollment among young men has declined from 47% to 42%. Meanwhile, the offshoring of manufacturing jobs—once a reliable pathway to the middle class for non-college-educated men—has further limited opportunities. Adding to these struggles is the growing unaffordability of housing: nearly 60% of men between the ages of 18 and 24 live with their parents, and even by age 30, one in five remains in their parents' home. Men are somewhat at sea and voted accordingly.

Also changing in the landscape of pride and achievement is the fact that we used to make things. It was in the pandemic that this really hit home. Suddenly, with the supply chain crisis we couldn't get the things that we wanted that we used to make in America. The pandemic was a significant awakening for many people, and it was reflected in how they voted.

Love or loath Mr. Trump, people voted for change. People voted for pain relief. People will mostly vote for their party, but if they are angry, they are compelled to do unpredictable things.

This book has no political agenda and makes no comment on who should or should not have won. If the other candidate had prevailed, I would be campaigning for the exact same thing. Presidents, power, and parties will always come and go, but if the family is properly represented, they will survive policy deviations, wars, economies, inflation, and the ever-changing vocational landscape.

To my point, the family crisis in America, on the surface, seems to have reached the finish line of crisis. A new direction in politics, whatever it is, generates positive sentiment, which is the most powerful economic driver of all. The first two years of any political term tend to reflect the effects of the last political term, so we don't really see the full effects of an administration until the third year. In this drastically changing political landscape, I anticipate that economic confidence will be initially very powerful. For right or wrong—with deregulation and the other types of sweeping change that this administration intends to implement—corporate and consumer confidence will drive an economic growth explosion. Gas and oil will flow, fuel costs will lessen, and the cost of living could become more manageable. Whether or not these policies are sustainable long-term, we will come to know, but consumer confidence is the driver, not necessarily what an administration does. It has been said 100 different ways that the president does not affect the stock market, and for the most part, that is true. It is the people who make investment decisions, and those decisions are usually made in response to positive or negative sentiment.

For me, I need to be a great dad, a great parent, a great provider, and a great citizen. No matter the election results four years from now, if we can get the Secretary of The Family in place and embed this new office in our culture, the family will endure any administration, and will set America on a new course of prosperity. It must be an untouchable office that the country cannot do without. Your vote—regardless of your candidate—was cast, no doubt, in the hope that your American family crisis could be over and that you will do better for your family than your parents did for you. That is the American dream. You made the right decision for you, and obviously, there are lots of Americans who agree and disagree with you, but one thing I think we all agree on is that the family should come first and be the central organism in our societal fabric. We have had a constant decline in the DNA that makes for a strong family for the entire lives of anyone alive today. This is because nobody is speaking up for the family as a central cause. Most of our discussions are about almost anything but the family.

The sentiment of the Americans in this election cycle who said, "enough is enough—you, the US government, need to start working for me. I earned it, I want it, and I deserve it—needs to be employed as ferociously in the direction of family resources to reconstruct what has been lost over the tens of decades of decline of the concept of family."

Aside from its polarizing brand effect, the sentiment of making America great again actually stands up, but I truly believe that the only way to actually achieve that is to make the American family great, which it has not been for as long as I can remember.

We must see to it that our diverse family values and our spiritual convictions have a place in our decision-making lives. We must reset our school curricula to include global and American history so we can grow as a reflection of what the past tells us is a better direction in life so we can make the American family great. The only federal education oversight should be to assure that basic standards of academic excellence are maintained. The states and local school boards should provide the leadership in all other parts of the academic experience. That would be fair, equitable, and put the family in control.

Do we, as citizens, now have the responsibility—not the government—to reinvigorate the emotional and psychosocial components of a community and a collective life in harmony?

The new administration promises that it is on a path to get back what it feels America has lost. For the family, we should define that for them:

1. The standard of living has diminished.
2. Opportunities for the middle and lower classes have been lessened.
3. Buying power has dwindled.
4. Education has been less of a powerful tool for making our kids smart.
5. Work–life balance.
6. Affordable home ownership.
7. Community engagement. (The decline of close-knit neighborhoods.)
8. Stable economic trajectories. (Long-term, stable careers have become less common.)
9. Traditional family roles and support. (Intergenerational support for child and elder care.)
10. Cultural continuity. (Passing down traditions.)
11. Interpersonal connection. (Digital disruption.)
12. If there were an incentive to have children, immigration would not be a consideration for population growth.

There was considerable debate in the run-up to the 2024 election regarding the southern border to the United States. The contention has been building for some time and parties were using it as a point of influence in their campaigning but let's examine this border contentiousness through the eyes of the family. Although our southern border has been an ongoing issue—and we are now taking steps to secure the border—we must be sensitive to the relationship between the jobs that migrants take and the need for workers to fill those jobs. Vital in our border closing process needs to be a dynamic relationship where there are jobs to be filled. Population growth statistics do not keep pace with the ability to fulfill these positions for the future. To do so, we must enhance the ability of the family to grow in number of children to satisfy job placements needed long term. This includes working with the private sector and our education departments at the high school and college levels to have educational programs for all skilled labor to infiltrate the job market.

The nature of education has changed dramatically to the point where a college degree is an expectation, and trades have been less and less integrated into the education process. Imagine if every school district across each state was required to have a trade school component. Each school would be required to provide evidence of exposure of the trades by incorporating trade education into its curricula for grades six, seven, eight, and nine. Those students who have a desire and aptitude for trades education, would then transfer to the trades school. An Ada Eric diploma is still available through a trades school. Trade schools would seek affiliations with trade unions, etc., for skills training, funding sources, and other support. This could level the family economic inequality in America.

It is widely known that only 40% of people who attend college are well suited to the higher learning that college offers and that 60%, although achieving graduation, leave college with no discernable, tangible skill or level of knowledge and understanding that can be employed in an aspirational vocational pursuit. We do have a lot of political science majors who may be better positioned to understand the political landscape or even run for politics but earning a living from such a degree is in many cases not even the intention. My point is that college has become a natural expectation from both parents and children. It is now rare not to go to college and there are excellent trades that can lead to success and fulfillment that are not being encouraged or pursued. The idea of engaging in a trade out of high school and pursuing higher education if desired is not normal and it can be. The country needs trades and other, presumably more desirable fields such as law, computer science, and finance are becoming more and more competitive, and trades are becoming harder to attract talent.

I'm presenting border and education points within the framework of the 2024 election chapter because we are at a major turning point and our directional objectives need to be clearly defined so that as we proceed through the ideas in this book to underpin the future of the American family, it will be done so through the lens of a new administration and the opportunities to install new thinking, new objectives, and new practices.

Mandate

I am proposing right here in the foundational arguments for the book that the new administration appoint a Secretary of the Family. It may develop into another title, but this person and office would review all agency policies and proposed or existing laws, to assure that the family stays firmly at the center of the decision-making and the objective be to achieve the prosperity and wellbeing for the American family. This will allow no family to be left behind by any government decision. It will assure that our economy reflects the need for growth of the family and the societal contributors, workers, and advocates it produces. It will assure that our education infrastructure provides diligence to knowledge, skills, and scholarship as needed by the families in their locations in the country, and to restore pride to being an American through the service of our government and its leadership. We will call this and any administration to the carpet to be held accountable to the people. The family.

3. PATERNITY LEAVE
CREATING A PERFECT STORM FOR CHANGE

*"A good father is one of the most unsung, unpraised, unnoticed, and
yet one of the most valuable assets in our society."*
—Billy Graham

Never one to accept the "accepted norms" in the world, as our second
child was developing in my wife's womb, I felt an intense pang. An
overwhelming emotion deep in my soul that would eventually drive me to
help effect change in the world.

Maternity leave for women was the accepted norm, but I was having
trouble accepting—because I had to work as a teacher—that I'd be generally
absent, as I was with the birth of our first child, from all the richness that
fatherhood brings. I'd miss experiencing all those firsts with my wife. I'd
already missed the opportunity to help her transition from wife—to wife
and mother.

You never get these moments back, and believe it or not, the development of children is such a finely balanced process that they can be perma-
nently affected by the slightest change. Even before these little souls present
themselves to the world, they are being affected by sound and emotion. This
is where family begins, and I didn't want to miss it—again.

Coming out of the 1960s and on a collision course with the 1970s, we
were in the depths of the Woodstock revolution when everything imag-
inable was feeling the force of change. Feminism, fairness, independence,
revolution, suffrage, and more. It was an epiphany. I jumped out of bed
and screamed, "Holy shit! Of course". It was a Betty Friedan—Gloria Stein
moment. Those iconic, catallactic women who had broken through impossible ceilings were inspiring me. Muriel Fox, Eleanor Pam, all of these inspiring people that had fought and were fighting for women, and suddenly I
said, well, you know, what about men? Not from the perspective of what
they had, but what they still didn't have, and I realized that there's reverse
discrimination when it came to paternity leave.

17

Every woman had the right to receive working compensation, but men did not. It was far from fair that our child would miss having a mother and a father at this important time, and if we really want to be on the side of families in America, paternity leave is a very good step.

Coupled to the feminist movement was my first daughter's urgent request of me one morning. As I was rushing to get out of the house and go to work (on time), she said, "Daddy, daddy, when you come home, can you bring me a rat?" I said, "What do you mean a rat?" "Well, you always say that there is a rat race you are going to. I want to see the rat."

I took that precedence to the New York City Board of Education and boldly exclaimed, "I want paternity leave!" "Are you crazy?" they said with uproarious laughter. It's never going to happen." I was a laughingstock. The idea was not part of history, philosophy, or the engagement of fairness that you would think would be in people's minds, particularly in education. So, I said, "All right, you don't want to give it to me, I'm going to sue you." In the end, that was not necessary.

* * *

Little did I know, right at the same time, a man who would later become a state senator and congressman, Gary Ackerman, was going through exactly the same experience. Back then, he was also in education. Mr. Ackerman was a teacher in New York City, and he and his wife had a daughter in late 1969. When his daughter reached 10 months old, he applied for leave (without pay) for childcare purposes.

As a resulting lawsuit played out, the principal of the school did not recommend to the district that Ackerman's application be approved; the superintendent, not surprisingly, followed suit by not approving the leave. After several unsuccessful appeals, Ackerman was again told that "childcare leave policies of the Board of Education only applied to female teachers."

Mr. Ackerman went somewhat rogue and simply disappeared from his job. He and his wife Rita filed a discrimination complaint with the Federal Equal Employment Opportunity Commission and sued the board in US district court. Their argument was that granting childcare leave only to women is an invasion of privacy because it forces mothers to be housekeepers and child rearers and prevents husbands and wives from dividing up family responsibilities as they see fit.

In 1973, the EEOC found that the mothers-only rule "discriminates against male teachers as a class." The board, as a result, said "it would reword its bylaws to ensure equal rights for fathers." The Board of Ed bylaws were amended so that it no longer referred to an affected teacher as "her" or relied on the timing of the teacher's pregnancy, thus expanding its relevancy to fathers and to adoptive parents. The determination is widely regarded as the groundbreaking first step toward paternity leave's existence.

The New York Board of Education was compelled to grant me four years. Steve Aiello was the president of the Board of Education at that time. Steve went on to the White House during the Carter administration to become President Carter's liaison on ethnic and urban affairs, while President Carter appointed me to the White House Conference on Families, where I served with many inspiring agents of change, including Coretta Scott King. In all honesty, though, nothing really transpired from that initiative to transform the country in a major way to think more about the family—it all became a little political. In fact, the tragedy is that here we are 40+ years later, and we still have not had another White House Conference on Families and it should be ignited along with bold proposals that are essential to get the American family out of a crisis and into an institution served by all we do. We talk a lot about gun legislation. We can pass K-12 basic education policies for our schools. All well and good, all important, but we're taking care of the fringe without focusing on the root cause, the nucleus of every issue worth fighting for—the American family. But as we will explore in this book, that story is not over. We will explore the White House Conference on Families in depth in a later chapter and propose how it could, and should, be reignited.

Win or lose, however, we must press on. All paternity wins aside, to this day, only 11 of our states have paid family leave legislation leaving a significant part of our country without this right. That's right, over 50 years after my historic paternity leave we still do not have a national paid family leave act. We fight on.

One of the big themes of our book here is nothing ever happens without remarkable effort. Massive catalytic change needs a massive catalyst. So many things needed to happen in a perfect storm for me to be awarded leave back in 1973, and none of those things would have mattered without wild and heretofore unseen acts of boldness.

Remember, if it weren't for the feminist movement, and my daughter asking for a rat, I would not have had the inspiration nor the compulsion to act in the way that I did. Paternity leave would never have been pursued by me. Perhaps, without Mr. Ackerman and me working together—even though we were not aware of each other's efforts—the New York Board of Education may not have felt enough pressure to rule in our favor. And because it was the New York Board of Education and not some smaller, less impactful organization, it became that big catalytic "magilla" that was needed to effect change.

In 2015, Sir Richard Branson was noted for creating a generous family leave policy for the Virgin Group, which included 12 months of paid leave for new dads. Others followed suit, such as Google, Netflix, and other Silicon Valley tech giants that viewed family leave as a valuable and deserved reward/incentive to encourage the loyalty and output of their employees.

Again, change may move slowly, but without giant, bold steps, it may never happen at all. It is time for federal paid leave for caregivers and this absolutely must be a central point on our agenda going forward. Evidence is showing a very positive trend for companies too. The benefits to employers are broad. One study found that in states with paid leave laws, employers saw a 5% increase in productivity compared with peer employers in states without such laws. Other research points to further benefits that enhance the bottom line. In New Jersey, for example, employers reported lower employee stress in relation to the state's paid family leave insurance program.

4. THE CURRENT STATE OF THE AMERICAN FAMILY

"The family is the nucleus of civilization."
— Will Durant

In an interview on Ottawa Public Television, distinguished Presidential Fellow in Urban Futures at Chapman University Joel Kotkin spoke in great detail on what he calls "The Rise of Post-Familialism, Humanity's Future." What is post-familialism? Well, basically, it is a phrase that describes how we may be moving away from a family-centric kind of society in which an increasing number of people choose not to get married and certainly not to have children.

The interviewer posed that it used to be all about family as portrayed in TV shows that embodied the norm; Leave It to Beaver, Father Knows Best, and even Happy Days. It was a simple formula, two adults, two kids and the world was built around it. But times are changing.

Dr. Kotkin maintained that the idea of the nuclear family is beginning to diminish in importance. This is a major phenomenon that is not just true in the United States but even more so in East Asia and Europe, and now we find it is beginning to become somewhat common in the developing world. When did this shift begin? Most likely in several stages.

We started to see these trends really express themselves during Japan's period of greater prosperity in the 1960s and 1970s. By the 80s people were not having children, and now this has spread to much of East Asia, Europe, the United States, and Canada as well.

Economics plays a powerful role. When you reach a certain level of prosperity on any trajectory, you generally have a lower birth rate; people are working, they're getting better educated, all basically good things.

Women are in the workforce, but then when you get to a certain level of prosperity and reach a tipping point, things start going sour, as they have in

---

*Sources: Pew Research Center, Census.gov, Survey Center on American Life.

Japan, as they are doing particularly in Southern Europe, as they have here in the United States. At that time, you start to see people delaying getting married and choosing not to have children. In this regard, economic prosperity may actually be better for the family than an economic depression. In Madrid, for example, we are seeing a radical drop in the number of marriages down to levels not seen since the 19th century.

Traditionally, there were many more what you might call blended families because people died. When they emigrated to the Great Plains, somebody might come from a small town in Scotland and migrate to Canada, going to live in Manitoba with an uncle or an aunt. So, we had this more blended kind of family, an extended family.

The 50s was really the heyday of this Leave it to Beaver family optic. In the 1960s and 1970s, with women getting into the workforce, becoming better educated, the sexual revolution, and the cultural changes of the 1960s, families began to lose some of their traditional patterns.

Today, we're seeing that really play out with ever-later marriage and lower birth rates.

Depending on the country, 20–30% are deciding simply never to have children in their lifetimes, not because they can't necessarily have children, but because either they won't have them, don't want to have them or feel they can't have them due to all sorts of phenomena such as high rents, the inability to purchase a single-family home, pressures from work. They're really different answers in almost every country we studied, but a lot of similarities.

Recent trends in the United States indicate a notable shift in family dynamics, with many individuals opting for pet ownership over having children. This change is influenced by various factors, including economic considerations, lifestyle preferences, and evolving societal norms. The United States has experienced a consistent decline in birth rates over recent years. In 2023, the number of births decreased to just under 3.6 million, marking the lowest count since 1979 and ending a brief increase observed during the late pandemic period. This decline was particularly notable among women under 40. Conversely, pet ownership has been on the rise. As of 2024, 66% of US households (approximately 86.9 million homes) own a pet, up from 56% in 1988. Dogs are the most popular pets, with 65.1 million households owning one, followed by cats in 46.5 million households. Of course, pets can't do the jobs needed long term so if our population is declining and our immigration reduces, we need a strategy for getting the work done. More babies are required. Unless of course AI reduces the need for many positions as it certainly promises to do. But it won't be able to fix plumbing or wire houses, etc. Much more about this in upcoming chapters.

"In Japan, they have a diminished workforce. This can manifest a lack of innovation in a society that lacks young people. This is one of the reasons why Japan has unexpectedly, to many people, fallen behind in the race to develop technology. I also think that there's a tremendous fiscal problem involved," Dr. Kotkin stated. In other words, you have fewer people working to support more retired people. This creates all sorts of problems for a society that has to support a nonworking population with an ever-shrinking base of people who are working. That's certainly one of the biggest effects.

There is a kind of spiritual effect. As people choose not to have children, the role of the family begins to change. Our perspective of what's important and what's not. As somebody who has children, it's hard to imagine what life would be without it. But more and more people are finding that they don't need to have children; that insurmountable desire that existed for generations is diminishing. That creates an ecosystem where not having children becomes ever more not only acceptable but even normative, particularly in specific kinds of environments.

If you were to map the predominance of this phenomenon, we could visualize the percentage of people without children and see that the inner core density has the lowest percentage of children. Then, it expands as you move further out from high-density metropolitan environments. So, if you have more and more people packed into the urban core, you will tend to have a much lower birth rate. Of course, there are many reasons for this, and it does not mean that people in densely populated urban centers are not starting families. With the space, services, and support structures that suburban environments provide, it is natural that young parents will choose to move to more conducive locations.

So, do we deliberately march back to the 1950s, as some have suggested? Well, that's not the way history works. But we have to start saying, okay, given that we support women in the workplace, for example—and let's face it, the cork is not going back in that bottle— and women moving into positions of authority, then the question is, how can we still preserve enough of a familial environment to sustain our society? It doesn't mean you have to go back to the 1950s even if you could, but I don't think you want to necessarily stay on a trajectory where 30–40% of your population does not have children.

In the same interview with Dr. Kotkin, Nora Spinks, the CEO of the Vanier Institute of the Family, added her perspective on the matter.

Ms. Spinks shared, and I'll paraphrase her remarks, that according to a recent census, only about 8% of families resembled the traditional family model. That is, the mother stays at home, the father goes to work, and the two kids are in suburbia in a single-family dwelling. But that doesn't make the other 90% of households not family. There are stepfamilies, blended families, gay marriages, and more. And with the conservative swing to enforcement of pro-life, if a gay couple is willing to raise a child that a heterosexual couple did not want to raise and they do a good job, why shouldn't they be complimented and supported for that?

We also have a new phenomenon of families that we refer to as LAT families, living alone together. They're married, but they're living in two houses.

Then we have LTA, living together and apart. This is where you've come together and formed a relationship; perhaps you're in your late 50s, and you've already been through one divorce; you don't want to do that again, but you've made a commitment to each other that you are now your chosen family, but you're going to keep your dwelling separate.

We must recognize that families are absolutely the cornerstone of our social and economic prosperity. Without families, we cannot function. Families, in all of their diversity, are critically important not only in individual households but also in neighborhoods and cities.

What we consider to be the traditional family—consisting of a married couple with children—now represents less than half of all US households. In 2022, married-couple households accounted for only 47% of households, a decline from 71% in 1970. At the same time, there is a rise in alternative family forms, such as cohabiting couples, single-parent households, and multigenerational families. The acceptance of these varied arrangements is growing, with a majority of Americans viewing single parenting, cohabitation, and same-sex parenting as acceptable family models.

Economic disparities continue to affect family structures. Married households generally report higher incomes and economic stability than single-parent families. Single mothers, in particular, face high rates of poverty, with 7.3 million single mothers in 2023, comprising over 80% of single-parent families. Financial strain is exacerbated by factors such as stagnant wages and the rising costs of childcare and housing. Additionally, low marriage rates among less-educated and lower-income individuals reflect a growing economic divide in family life.

Attitudes toward marriage are also changing. Fewer Americans view marriage as essential for a fulfilling life, and the percentage of adults who have never married is at an all-time high. The share of children living with two married parents has dropped significantly, from 67% in 1970 to 37% in recent years. At the same time, domestic roles within households are evolving, with significant disparities in the division of labor between genders, especially among households with children. Women continue to bear a greater share of domestic responsibilities, which can affect relationship satisfaction and work–life balance.

These trends highlight an ongoing transformation in American family life. Addressing the challenges and supporting diverse family structures will be crucial for fostering resilience and economic stability among American families. For further information, you may explore comprehensive reports from the Pew Research Center and the U.S. Census Bureau, which provide deeper insights into these ongoing changes.

Comparing American families to those around the world reveals notable differences in family structures, economic impacts, and social roles, which can highlight both advantages and challenges unique to the United States.

For example, American households tend to be smaller than those in regions like Sub-Saharan Africa and parts of Asia, where multigenerational households are common. For instance, average household sizes in the United States are around 2.5 people, whereas countries like Senegal have averages exceeding eight people per household. This smaller household size in the United States often leads to a focus on the nuclear family, whereas in other regions, extended families play a larger role in caregiving and economic support. Countries with larger household sizes often have strong family networks that provide resilience against economic and social challenges, which can sometimes be lacking in the more individualistic American family structure.

Globally, countries with strong family-supportive policies often have better family stability. For example, many European countries offer extensive parental leave, affordable childcare, and universal healthcare, which helps reduce economic stress on families. In contrast, American families frequently struggle with high childcare costs, limited parental leave, and healthcare expenses. Nordic countries, in particular, have robust family support systems, which contribute to higher levels of family well-being and work–life balance. These countries' policies enable both parents to work or share responsibilities, which is less common in the United States, where economic pressures often push both parents into full-time work or force one to stay at home due to childcare costs.

There is also a divergence in societal acceptance of different family structures. In the United States, single-parent and same-sex families are more accepted compared to some more conservative regions. However, American society remains somewhat divided on issues like cohabitation and marriage. Other countries, particularly in Scandinavia, show higher levels of acceptance for diverse family arrangements, including cohabitation and single parenting, which are supported by social policies that treat all family forms equally.

The United States lags behind many European countries regarding gender equality in household responsibilities. In countries like Sweden and Denmark, there is a more equal division of household labor between genders, supported by policies that encourage both parents to engage equally in childcare and household tasks. In the United States, women still tend to bear a greater share of domestic duties, which can affect their participation in the workforce and contribute to gender inequality.

Globally, many developed countries, including the United States, face declining fertility rates and aging populations. Japan and Italy, for example, have extremely low birth rates and an increasing number of elderly citizens, creating challenges in sustaining their economies and social services. The United States has a slightly higher fertility rate compared to some of these countries, but it still faces challenges related to an aging population and the economic burden of care.

Overall, countries with comprehensive family support policies often show more favorable outcomes for families, including better gender equality, stronger economic resilience, and higher levels of family stability. By examining global practices, the United States can improve family well-being through policies that support diverse family structures, work–life balance, and economic security.

* * *

The perspectives of Dr. Kotkin and Ms. Spinks, which we explored earlier in this chapter, inform us significantly and help provide a foundational stance for this book's arc.

In summary, over the past hundred years, the idea of family has changed in ways that are far from superficial. These changes have come about as a result of great shifts in society, as lauded by many as the long-overdue arrival of a more enlightened era. For many, the traditional family model—a husband and wife, both of whom engage in parenting and living with their biological children—has remained firmly lodged in their imaginations as the ideal family. However, the "ideal" is rarely realized in actual lived experience, and what counts as "family" in the United States today encompasses a dizzyingly wide range of forms, roles, and arrangements.

How we communicate in families has been redefined in the digital age. We are always on the phone; we text instead of talk, and we swim in the social media pool like it were daily exercise. If only we exercised that much. On the positive side, I not only keep in touch with my own family in a way that we couldn't or didn't before but also with extended family. Because of the changes in digital platforms and their positive and negative effects on our lives, we are yet to see how these new behaviors will play out in our futures. The psychological and sociological impacts are hard to imagine, but I'm not sure any of them will make us happier or more well-rounded as a species. Or maybe I'm wrong. Maybe it will lead to telepathic communication, and we will all know what each other is thinking, forcing us to be constantly considerate of our thoughts. Alas, the mind wanders.

Moreover, the emergence of telecommuting and the digital nomad lifestyle might also influence family structures—allowing for even more living arrangements that defy the traditional structure of a home and potentially giving rise to alternative family models as societal attitudes toward home and family continue to shift. What seems certain is that the very idea of a family—what constitutes a family, what it means to be a family—is evolving.

As these alternative family models become more commonplace, the impact that families have on the lives of their members (and on society in general) is likely to remain a potent force that, in some way or another, defines or redefines the nature of our society and influences its endurance.

* * *

One recent and important catalyst for familial change was experienced during and after the COVID-19 pandemic. Not only was the pandemic a major health crisis, but it was also an instigator for many social changes, including—quite profoundly—the structures we think of as families. When people were forced into isolation, it tested all kinds of relationships. The unprecedented nature of the pandemic allowed people to think outside the box of what a family is. While separations resulted in some cases, others found ways to connect that showed just how resilient human beings can be when it comes to finding and creating relationships that are meaningful.

It is also worthy of note that the relationships that ended were most likely already stressed to the point of cracking and the forced isolation of the pandemic was the straw that broke the marriage's back.

During the initial stage of the pandemic, the forms of societal interaction that people had long taken for granted—the handshake, the hug, and so on—had to be abandoned. We were told to spend as little time as possible in the presence of anyone not part of our immediate family—that is, anyone not already in the home we shared. We were told to get used to being alone with our immediate families for long stretches of time.

Most of us didn't have much of a choice. Confined together in our homes, the people we lived with became our last, best hope for maintaining our sanity. As if we didn't have enough on our plates already, the parents in these households were now expected to take up the instructional slack on a day-to-day basis, not to mention the work that clearly could not be put on hold.

Introspection and bonding have been pushed along by the pandemic, but bonding seems to be the more accurate term. Certainly, many people have sat down to do a little more pondering than usual. However, the main thrust of the pandemic has been—at least for those fortunate enough to maintain their health and livelihood—a forced pause in the hectic day-to-day life that many people used to lead. Once again, families had the opportunity to reconnect and get to know each other again. Cooking, game nights, and other wholesome activities took the place of what used to pass for family time in normal (pre-pandemic) times.

The pandemic pushed us to rethink what a family is. With everyone spread out and our physical interactions so limited, the old image of the family took a hit. In its place, many of us turned—not to the old neighborhood—but to families of friends that we chose. In some cases, neighbors and community members became, in essential ways, our supports and companions. Some shine a light on this aspect of the pandemic by saying it has made us realize that family isn't just about biology. And that's a family we can all support.

Additionally, the crisis brought to light the specific challenges encountered by single-parent households, multi-generational families, and individuals living alone. The pandemic emphasized how much we depend on social support and even on the pretense of social support, leading the nation to an increased reliance on virtual interfaces as that which feels like "normal" just didn't exist anymore. As we became used to the alternate reality of "normal" in our pre-VR world, many of us found that our digital lives became even more of a "lifeline" than before. In the end, I would argue that our digital lives became a bigger part of our sense of community in 2020 than they had previously.

As the pandemic developed, the idea of caregiving gained newfound depth and complexity. With the healthcare system overwhelmed and the elderly especially at risk, many families found themselves shouldering the kinds of responsibilities that we would ordinarily associate with caregiving. They found themselves learning to manage complicated, daily tasks that kept their loved ones safe and healthy. Many of us stepped into these roles without really signing up for them or even having the right training.

The existing inequalities within family structures were certainly laid bare by the pandemic. The intense and accelerated nature of the caregiving demands made the mid-stages of the pandemic a hallmark for women's lives. Many women found themselves pushed into the caregiving role in a way that was not only traditional but also regressive, leading them to sacrifice career ambitions and mental health. Men's role in family caregiving was largely absent from this experience, even though more men than ever are capable of and willing to share this responsibility.

As the world slowly pulled free of the pandemic's hold, the transformations it brought about in family structures became apparent. Quite a few families emerged from the experience with newfound strengths, having together weathered the trials of necessary isolation and a world turned upside down. The resilience earned through living under the cloud of a global emergency—an 8- to 10-month family survival challenge—seems likely to influence family forms and relations for years to come.

The COVID-19 pandemic was a change agent, molding and shaping family life into something else within a relatively short timeframe, which shows that drastic short-term change is indeed possible given the right circumstances.

The pandemic took the old ideas about family and rearranged them. The notions of family that some people held were actively challenged by the situation. For many, the pandemic stressed the idea that your vital connections don't have to occur only along biological lines or even within the "traditional" family structure. The situation prompted people to rethink what family is, to consider whom they're really close to, and to re-evaluate the importance of all sorts of relationships in their lives.

* * *

Finally, to round out our foundational structure for this book, we must talk about the demise of "the village." The shift from large extended family units to small nuclear families has greatly changed family life and the dynamics of support, caregiving, and social interaction. In the "village" way of living—where multiple generations and relatives lived in proximity—families enjoyed a powerful network of shared duties and assets. That living arrangement made for a strong sense of belonging and security in that children were raised not just by their parents but by a community of caregivers who delivered the same kind of values and traditions parents do.

The shift toward nuclear families seems to have led directly toward the isolation of the nucleus and a reduced support system. Instead of drawing on a wide circle of family members or even old friends, many mothers and fathers are figuring it all out without delegating tasks or leaning on others for emotional or instrumental support. Parenting has become what psychologists call an "all-consuming" endeavor; you can't do it right at a distance or without being highly attentive. To make matters worse, the supposed friends and neighbors that turned up in old sitcoms to complement family life have all but vanished. In this book, we will explore where our frameworks of families came from, how they changed over time, where we are now, and where we are likely to head as a result of technology, politics, attitudes, ideals, and more.

Current research conducted by Pew shows that the public is more pessimistic than optimistic about various aspects of American life. See the following chart for sentiment percentages.

Subject	Pessimistic	Optimistic	Neutral
The moral and ethical standards in our country	63	16	16
Our country's system of education	59	20	17
Our country's ability to ensure racial equality for all people*	44	28	23
Our country's ability to get along with other countries**	41	30	24
The Institution of marriage and the family	40	25	29

5. THE IRON AGE AND THE AGE OF ENLIGHTENMENT
(HOW DID WE GET HERE?)

"Out of the crooked timber of humanity, no straight thing was ever made."
— Immanuel Kant

To get a true sense of our historical and familial arc, we need to start at a place where we can begin to track the changes and monitor the forces of such change.

The Iron Age marks a significant period in human history, characterized by the widespread use of iron for tools and weapons. Beginning around 1200 BCE and lasting until the early centuries CE, the Iron Age followed the Bronze Age and brought profound changes to ancient societies.

For example, the advent of iron smelting and forging revolutionized technology as well as daily life. Iron tools were harder and, therefore, more durable than their bronze counterparts, enabling more efficient agriculture, improved craftsmanship, and stronger weapons. This technological leap facilitated population growth, urbanization, and the expansion of trade networks.

In Europe, the Iron Age saw the rise of prominent cultures such as the Celts, who spread across the continent, leaving a legacy of intricate metalwork and fortified settlements. In the Near East, the Hittites were among the first to develop ironworking techniques, and they, in turn, influenced neighboring civilizations. Meanwhile, in India and China, advancements in iron metallurgy contributed to the emergence of powerful states and sophisticated societies.

The Iron Age also witnessed significant social and political transformations. The increased availability of iron weapons altered the nature of warfare, leading to the rise of new military strategies and the downfall of established powers. Societies became more hierarchical, with powerful chieftains and kings controlling vast territories and resources.

Cultural and religious practices evolved during this era, often intertwined with the use of iron. Ironworking itself was sometimes regarded with mystique, believed to hold magical properties. Myths and legends from this period reflect the awe and reverence for the metal that shaped the age.

The Iron Age laid the groundwork for subsequent historical developments, setting the stage for classical antiquity and the rise of great empires such as Rome. It was a time of innovation, conflict, and transformation, leaving an indelible mark on the course of human civilization.

⋆ ⋆ ⋆

The changes that came with the shift from the Bronze Age to the Iron Age transformed not only the economic basis of life but also family dynamics, daily patterns, and the division of responsibilities within households. Life in families became more involved in certain ways and less in others. The very nature of ironworking began to change. No longer simply a cottage industry, ironworking took on specializations and the scale of a craft. Certain family members, especially males, began to assume prominent roles as blacksmiths and metalworkers, amassing goods and serving local economies. Ironworking specialization sometimes led to the formation of family workshops and, by the end of the Iron Age, a family-operated metal industry.

The appearance of iron weapons and the necessity for armament gave rise to war. War strengthened patriarchal structures. It gave authority to men who were seen as warriors. These men were better perceived as heads of households because they took on the "manly" role of protector—of both family and community. The tools and weapons of iron, however, required more than just a male figure for their operation; they also necessitated larger family units and community structures. This was because the resources, both human and material, required to establish and maintain those larger units and that community structure were, ironically, unlike iron, more basic and more readily available in the Stone Age.

Iron tools allowed the people of the time to work with the soil more easily and effectively. Despite the increase in land needing to be managed due to the upsurge in food production, the people of that time almost certainly found existence to be less demanding day-to-day. Even with the shift to more of an agricultural lifestyle, the roles that women played continued to be essential in making life run smoothly. Along with cultivating their land, the families of that time also began to take up more of an emphasis on home-building and property management.

The cultural and religious practices of ancient societies were influenced by iron's seemingly magical qualities. Households may have used iron in their rituals, believing it to have life-giving and protective powers, much as they might have used their very ingenious knowledge of metallurgy to potentiate their charms and amulets. Knowledge of ironworking—a trade, incidentally, that was vital in ancient times for its power to change farm implements and tools—had to be transmitted from family member to family member. Elders, especially those skilled in the use of iron, took on prominent roles as educators in their societies.

Although men became more visible in war and metalwork, it was women who held the family together in the farming and home front. Women's work in agriculture, textile production, and household management was vital and could only grow in importance as the family unit became even more of a necessity at this key period. The increasing complexity of the household and the farm sometimes meant that the adolescent and even preadolescent children of the family assumed more of the not-yet internships, learning the rudiments of the essential work served by the women of the family.

Taken as a whole, the move to the Iron Age caused sweeping changes that struck at the very heart of families, life within them, and the structures that surround them. The first of these changes was wrought by a series of technological advancements that sharpened tools and weapons and made them more efficient and effective. These improvements in technology had far-reaching effects that spilled over into the economic realm.

＊　＊　＊

From Iron to Enlightenment

The late 17th century to the 18th century was, in human history, a long moment that pivoted on thought, emphasizing reason, individualism, and empirical evidence over tradition and religious dogma. Of course, the movement of Enlightenment stretched—not in a smooth line—throughout Europe and across the ocean to America, where it found fertile ground for a reorganization of the landscape of philosophy, politics, and science. One of its profound changes amongst the young states was providing a boost to the reformation of European family structures.

Within this agrarian framework of the Iron Age, marriage was frequently seen not as a romantic partnership but as a binding together of two families with a similar social and economic status in a form of alliance that was perhaps best described as a familial "fusion." In this context, the word marriage meant alliance and that children born of the alliance were heirs and "continuators of the 'fused' families." Moreover, marriage preserved and passed on not just lineage but also property, titles, and accomplishments.

The Enlightenment was a much-needed occasion for a radical reconsideration of human relationships and for an equally radical routing of the established norms of the Iron Age. For too long, philosophers had viewed family life through the lens of the Iron Age norms of human life. In the era of economic man, state power, and human survival, philosophers like John Locke and Jean-Jacques Rousseau came close to recognizing the essential partnership that marriage was a relationship of equality between partners who might not have been much in love.

The most substantial overall change during this time was the movement toward the current family structures. The term "nuclear" as it pertains to the American perception began in the 1920s when the academic fields of anthropology and sociology were both still young, but its etymology dates back 250 years from its parent word, nucleus, which had been used to describe the condensation of the family to its more modern context.

As more people moved into the cities, the economy became predominantly urban, and families sought better opportunities in towns and cities; the agrarian family economy mostly disappeared. In its place, the nuclear family had become an almost universal structure that lent itself to greater emotional and private intimacy, as well as individual autonomy, within the family. In part, this was because the nuclear family was, in essence, a smaller family that had fewer faces and voices in its different rooms; you could hear everyone almost anywhere with your ears or see almost everyone with your eyes.

The families' dynamics transformed under the Enlightenment's push for reason and education. The importance of learning was even more magnified in families, with an increased emphasis on nurturing that was both head and heart centered. Head-centered people tend to be more cerebral and fact-based. They are logical and also good at problem-solving—until they aren't, and that's usually when they get rigid and controlling with their rules for the way life must be lived. Heart-centered people are more emotionally fluent and comfortable with the realm of feelings and intuitions. They are also more connected to their authentic selves and, sometimes, more connected to their dreams and true desires.

Even when the head-centered model of learning for children was dominant, the heart freshened up the atmosphere in which individual expression and even some limited forms of "family criticism" became possible. Some forms of this model still had son-and-daughter forms, appearing in both prose and poetry, sometimes with vigor, sometimes with quiet intensity.

The Enlightenment was a truly momentous time in human history that turned human thought and social structures—especially those of the family—upside down. When one contrasts the inflexible, patriarchal family structures of the Iron Age with the more adaptable, egalitarian ones that emerged in the wake of the Enlightenment, the truly transformative power of this intellectual movement becomes even more evident. The Enlightenment is a foundational moment for our modern constructs of individuality, rights, and emotional partnerships in marriage. Carrying on from what the authors of the Enlightenment articulated, we have gradually reshaped the family to be more of a partnership than a hierarchy.

6. THE NATURE OF FAMILY

"In every conceivable manner, the family is a link to our past,
a bridge to our future."
— Alex Haley

The towering Greek philosopher Aristotle, who lived in the 4th century BCE, had a hand in many fields of thought, such as ethics, metaphysics, and politics. Despite this, he is perhaps best known for his many profound and penetrating insights into the nature of "familial" relationships, especially those that involve parents, children, and siblings. Although he wrote less directly about such associations, Aristotle had equally insightful things to say about the nature of marital relationships. He also professed with great frequency and fervor the fundamental importance of the family as a social unit and association for both the natural and moral cultivation of its members. Indeed, Aristotle's thinking about the family is as socially relevant today as it was in the late 4th century BCE.

The concept of the family, as Aristotle understood it, emphasizes the even exchange between parents and children and the shared responsibilities that bind family members together. In Aristotle's ethical framework, the family is the first and most important society—"one's nearest and dearest." The foundation of every family is the principle of reciprocity, which involves not only the even exchange that makes the family a life-sustaining community but also the deep moral obligation family members have to one another. The family, in Aristotle's view, is a microcosm of society, where the principles that make family life fulfilling also make society life-lasting.

In the family setting, Aristotle underscores the value of roles and pecking orders, positing that each member has certain obligations that, if performed well, contribute to the whole. He and she (the husband and wife) perform in different yet complementary ways. Each sets the kind of home environment that is propitious for the kind of kids who become rulers later on. The home is where the children learn to be virtuous, and the "interdependence" (as it is sometimes called) of mom and dad in fulfilling their different but go-to roles is the main ingredient in the family staying together and both kids and parents being happy.

In addition, Aristotle maintains that the family represents the first and most immediate human association. He sees the family as the setting in which the precepts of justice can be imparted to individuals, who then carry these precepts into the wider society. For Aristotle, the family is where moral education begins—not in a schoolroom but at home, around the dinner table. By learning to practice reciprocity with their family members, children learn the kind of character that makes them good citizens.

Aristotle also understood the family to be an institution on which the very existence of the state depended. In his mind, it was the first society, the first structure of governance. From it, just as from the family tree, extends the branches of all other societies.

Aristotle placed the family at the heart of something he called "the political man." His argument has already been made in *The Family*, a book by the esteemed scholar David L. McCullough. But allow me, if you will, to repeat some of McCullough's strokes and, in part, to draw on his authority to vex a rather large bee in the rather large bonnet of contemporary political discourse. While virtues such as justice and courage, to say nothing of the virtues of the political man in the hub of the home, have not been up for grabs since the early 1960s, the family has been up for grabs a lot longer than that.

Aristotle sketches the family, with specific attention to its roles. He makes clear the hierarchy of its members and how each one functions. He sees three main roles: the husband, the wife, and the children. The husband is the "head," a term Aristotle does not use but which is implied. He sees the husband as the one who should make the large decisions: the ones impacting not just the day-to-day life of the family but it's very future. He sees the household as something that, day to day, must be managed. He sees the wife as the one who properly manages it, with the husband being away much of the time. "The husband is to provide the family's primary source of income," he states, and doesn't comment much on why this is a good thing. Still, we can guess: the husband is doing this on account of being virtuous.

Aristotle extends his view of family beyond appearance; he looks at the emotional and ethical dimensions of family relationships. He emphasizes the critical nature of friendship, or philia, in the family. He believes that "genuine affection and mutual respect among family members" is necessary for a virtuous life. Obviously, the kind of life his Ethics encourages is one in which members strive together to be good, to be virtuous. And if one is virtuous, one is kind, compassionate, and even forgiving (though it is obviously not easy at times to forgive). Benito interprets Aristotle as saying that the family unit provides the "nurturance necessary to foster virtues" and that the "benefits of family life extend well beyond personal development."

Aristotle understands that families have problems just like any other social unit, especially in maintaining the kind of harmony and balance that is essential for their good functioning. He is certainly aware that interests and desires quite different from one another may and do cause conflicts between family members and that these conflicts can and do escalate into real disputes. At the same time, he believes that most family conflicts are easily resolved because they are not really about interests and desires but are instead virtuous teaching moments poorly handled.

To sum up, Aristotle's perception of the family is intricate. The philosopher's basic premise is that the family plays an instrumental role in both private and public life, allowing individuals unfettered paths toward the attainment of self-governance and the realization of a virtuous life. Aristotle's vision of the family, with its special and valuable organizational form, is in stark contrast to the modern liberal perception of it. Such a perception seems to view the organization of the family as a mere ad hoc association and also an unfurled path toward modern family life. When modern individuals look to the past, they sometimes perceive the family, like the life course it organizes, as a thing of the past and something to be nostalgized over.

The illustrious 18th-century philosopher Immanuel Kant, on the other hand, is known primarily for the importance he placed on metaphysics, epistemology, and ethics. But Kant's understanding of families—while perhaps not as exhaustively worked out as his systems of more traditional philosophical themes—matters. For Kant, the family was a critical institution, playing the kind of role that might be thought of as the "cultivation" of virtue and moral kinds of reasoning, "for" (in his words) "the family is the first society, and a person therein receives the first lessons in moral conduct, which forms the basis of all subsequent lessons in the kinds of reasoning that make a person a good citizen."

Kant's ethical framework centers around the idea that individuals' moral capacities are first developed in the family. He believed that children learn the essential principles of duty, respect, and love within the family unit and that children's interactions with their parents (and with other authority figures) establish the all-important sense of obligation that Kant thought was the foundation of any individual's moral life. In Kant's eyes, the family is much more than a social unit; it is a "moral community" where individuals are nurtured and guided in their pursuit of an ethical life.

Kant gave great attention to the family as a domain for the exercise of autonomy and rationality. His contention was that even though relationships in the family are filled with affection and love and are, in fact, models of such things, they should also, in Kant's words, be "educational." What he meant by that is something like this: the family ought to be a place where the young are prepared, in a way suited to their capacities and in a way that no one else could really do, to become independent moral agents.

To sum up, Kant placed a high value on the family. He saw it as a crucial context for moral upbringing and the development of ethical individuals. He believed that individuals learn duty and respect within the family. These are the two principles that he held as being central for just societies. He insisted that it is within the family, and only within the family, that individuals can learn both principles.

Sigmund Freud viewed the family as a central institution in shaping an individual's psychological development. He believed that early family relationships, particularly those involving parents, play a critical role in the formation of personality and the unconscious mind. Freud emphasized the importance of family dynamics, such as the Oedipus complex, where a child's feelings of attachment, rivalry, and identification with parents influence their emotional and social growth. Ultimately, the family serves as the foundational arena where fundamental conflicts and desires are experienced and negotiated, leaving lasting impressions on an individual's psyche.

Harry Stack Sullivan viewed the family as a crucial environment for shaping interpersonal relationships and mental health. He emphasized that the family acts as the primary context in which a person learns patterns of communication, emotional exchange, and social interaction. Sullivan believed that the quality of early relationships within the family, particularly with caregivers, significantly influences the development of self-esteem, security, and the ability to form meaningful connections with others. Through these interactions, individuals acquire the tools for navigating the broader social world and managing their emotional well-being.

Carl Jung viewed the family as a fundamental influence on an individual's psychological development, emphasizing the interplay between personal experiences and inherited collective elements. He introduced the concept of the "family complex," suggesting that unresolved issues and emotional patterns within a family can significantly impact a person's psyche. Jung believed that children are not "blank slates" but inherit the collective experiences of humanity, as well as the specific dynamics of their family history.

He also proposed that the family serves as a primary context where archetypes—universal, inherited symbols and patterns—manifest and influence behavior. Through the process of individuation, individuals work to integrate these familial and archetypal influences, striving to develop a balanced and whole personality.

Alfred Adler viewed the family as a vital setting for shaping a person's personality and social orientation. He believed that early family experiences, including sibling relationships and parental attitudes, play a significant role in forming an individual's sense of belonging, self-worth, and social interest. Adler emphasized the influence of birth order, suggesting that a person's position within the family impacts their behavior, ambitions, and coping strategies. Ultimately, the family serves as the initial context where individuals learn cooperation, develop their goals, and establish the foundation for their lifelong interactions with others.

The views of Freud, Sullivan, Jung, Adler, Aristotle, and Kant on the family align in recognizing its central role in shaping individuals, though their emphases and philosophical underpinnings differ. Here's a comparative breakdown of their alignments and conflicts:

Points of Alignment

1. The Family's Role in Development:
   All six thinkers agree that the family profoundly influences individual development. For Freud, the family is key to psychological development through unconscious dynamics; Sullivan sees it as foundational for interpersonal relationships; Jung emphasizes the impact of family archetypes and inherited patterns; Adler highlights its role in shaping social interest and personality; Aristotle considers it central to ethical and character formation; and Kant views it as a moral institution fostering the development of virtues.

2. Family as a Social Unit:
   Aristotle, Kant, and Adler see the family as the basic unit of society, where individuals learn cooperation and responsibility. Freud, Sullivan, and Jung indirectly support this by acknowledging the family's role in preparing individuals for broader social interactions.

3. Ethical and Emotional Influence:
   Aristotle and Kant focus on the ethical responsibilities of family life, while Freud, Sullivan, Jung, and Adler emphasize emotional and psychological influences. These perspectives converge on the idea that family shapes both internal character and external behavior.

Points of Conflict

1. Focus on the Individual vs. Society:
   Freud, Sullivan, Jung, and Adler focus on the individual's development and psychological needs within the family. In contrast, Aristotle and Kant prioritize the family's role in shaping ethical and social virtues for the good of society.

2. Nature of Influence:
   Freud emphasizes unconscious conflicts (e.g., the Oedipus complex) and their lifelong impact, while Jung focuses on archetypal and inherited patterns. Adler diverges by stressing conscious, goal-directed behavior and the family's role in fostering social interest. Sullivan, meanwhile, highlights interpersonal dynamics and communication within the family.
   Aristotle and Kant do not delve into unconscious or psychological processes, instead focusing on rationality, ethics, and duty within family relationships.

3. Theoretical Foundations:
   Aristotle and Kant operate within ethical and philosophical frameworks, emphasizing rational and moral principles. Freud, Sullivan, Jung, and Adler rely on psychological theories, often delving into nonrational processes, like the unconscious (Freud and Jung) or interpersonal dynamics (Sullivan).

4. Birth Order and Family Roles:
   Adler uniquely emphasizes birth order and sibling relationships as determinants of personality, a concept not explored by the others.

5. Transcendental vs. Practical Views:
   Jung introduces a spiritual and collective dimension to the family's influence, with archetypes extending beyond the immediate family to

humanity as a whole. This contrasts with Aristotle and Kant, who remain focused on the practical, societal, and moral roles of the family.

Summary of Alignment and Conflict

While these thinkers agree on the importance of the family, their perspectives diverge based on their foundational interests: Freud's psychoanalysis, Sullivan's interpersonal focus, Jung's archetypal psychology, Adler's social orientation, Aristotle's virtue ethics, and Kant's moral philosophy. These differences reflect their broader theoretical commitments but underscore a shared belief in the family as a cornerstone of individual and societal development.

Freud's ideas may be the most culturally pervasive overall, while Aristotle remains dominant in philosophical discussions.

* * *

The family dynamic in America is changing. We're moving away from the traditional family and instead seeing more complex structures arise in American homes. We are seeing a lot more diversity in family types (and they're not so different from one another as some might think).

We're also seeing, at least in some parts of America, a lot more diversity in the skin shades of the children who call these homes "home." And all of this happened—from the increased complexity of families to the increased shades of color in families—within less than 50 years. In 1960, over 85% of kids lived with both parents. Now it's less than 70%. Adjusted for the amount of poverty that's now in America, the 1960 figures look a lot better than today's.

These trends have given rise to a dizzying array of family forms, which are now supplanting the one-time dominant family structure in the United States. In the year 1960, at the apogee of the baby boom, we lived in what was essentially a one-family nation. An astounding 73% of all children lived with two married parents in their first sensible marriage. This figure had dropped to 61% by 1980, and today it is less than half. Meanwhile, children living with cohabiting parents are now counted among the variety of family forms. The constancy that characterized family living arrangements has eroded.

For example, nearly 31% of kids below 6 years old saw their family structure change drastically, with parental divorce, separation, or cohabitation in just three years. Of the children living with two parents, a significant number of them have seen at least one episode of their family living in a different arrangement—from living together as a married couple, to separation, or even divorce, and then a return to living together. Today, only 62% of children under 18 live with two married parents, which is a record low.

On the other hand, the percentage of children brought up by a single parent has risen to 26%. That represents almost a quarter of all children. Divorce is clearly a major factor in that increase. Today, almost half of all first marriages (44%) are expected to end in divorce. Men and women who have been through it generally say that it was one of the most difficult experiences of their lives. If we divide children into two groups—those who are in single-parent homes and those who are in two-parent homes—we find that the kids in two-parent homes generally score higher on measures of well-being.

Of the cohort of children currently in the United States, less than half—46%—are being raised in a home with two married biological parents, a reality that is far from universal in the United States. This traditional setup of marriage and childrearing is declining geometrically; children in two-parent households—biological or adopted—represent a figure that now stands at about 55%. However, while the proportion of children in single-parent homes has increased systems of care and proportion of homes for children with neither parent have been steady. Approximately 5% of children are being raised by a relative in the absence of parents.

The structure of families differs widely by race and level of education. The majority of white, Hispanic, and Asian kids grow up in two-parent households. Among them, Asian children have the highest percentage living with both parents: 84%. Among white children, 78% live with both parents. When we lump together all the kids who are in the Hispanic category, 66% have both parents present. Black children are the least likely to live in a two-parent setting. Even though 46% of Black kids do live with both parents or with a cohabiting couple, only 22% of Black children live with two parents who are both in their first marriage.

Family structure is also affected by the education that parents have received. Children with at least one college-educated parent are far more likely to live in two-parent households. They are also far more likely to have parents who are in their first marriage. And when we exclude the three million children living with an unmarried or gay couple, three million children living with a single parent, and the three million children living in foster care, the figures for the "intact family" are really pretty good across the board. Blended families, where children live with a stepparent, stepsibling, or half-sibling, make up 16% of households.

Families in the United States have been getting smaller. A steady decline in fertility rates has contributed to this trend. Although family sizes decreased for all racial and ethnic groups during the 1990s and 2000s, the most recent recession had a particularly pronounced effect on African American families, prompting a significant decline in the number of children mothers in that community have. While only 4% of mothers with a bachelor's degree had four or more children in 2010, 20% of mothers with a high school diploma or less did. And half of the Hispanic mothers surveyed in 2011 had three or more children, compared to just 27% of Asian mothers.

In much the same way, less-educated women tend to have more children. Women not only have fewer children than in the past but also have children under quite different circumstances. The past association of childbearing with marriage has weakened, with a dramatic increase in nonmarital births. In 1960, only 5% of births occurred outside of marriage, but by 2005, this figure had risen to 37.3%, with even more recent figures suggesting the percentage was closer to 40%.

A child is more likely to experience instability if their parents live together but are not married. Cohabiting unions are less stable than marriages. About 50% of children born to cohabiting parents will see their parents separate before the child turns 9. In contrast, only 20% of children born to married parents experience parental separation. Births to unmarried women are most common among women with fewer educational credentials. While only 11% of new mothers with a college degree were unmarried in 2014, a whopping 54% of high school-educated new mothers were unmarried.

Having children with multiple partners is increasingly common among certain demographic groups, especially blacks, Hispanics, and those with less formal education. Almost 20% of women in their childbearing years report having had at least one child with a partner who is not the child's other biological parent—this means that nearly 20% of women will have lived the life of a mother without something close to half of the first two decades of that child's life. Today's parents are less likely to be married but more likely to be older and better educated. The average age of a new mother has risen sharply in just the last decade, let alone the last generation.

Contemporary mothers have a much higher rate of participation in higher education. Whereas only 18% of the mothers of infants in 1960 had attended any amount of college, by the year 2000, at least 67% of the mothers of infants had some college experience. The workforce participation of mothers has also increased dramatically. In 1975, only 47% of mothers with children under 18 were in the labor force; by 2000, this figure had risen to 73%. The most recent available figures from the U.S. Bureau of Labor Statistics show that 70% of mothers with children under 18 are employed, with about three-quarters of these mothers working full-time.

A mother's education level has a strong correlation with her likelihood of being in the labor force. Nearly half of all mothers who have not graduated high school (49%) are employed, a number that bumps up to 65% for mothers who hold a high school diploma and to 79% for those who have attained a 4-year college degree. Not only are mothers now working in higher numbers, but a growing share of them are the ones bringing home the bacon.

Currently, 40% of families with children under 18 have a mother who leads as the primary earner; in 1960, only 11% of families had a mother who was the primary earner. Earners counted in those figures are mothers who are single or have partners. Among partnered families, about half of the couples in dual-income families are seen as part of that "rise of mothers" narrative. "Stay-at-home moms" is a term applied to mothers who do not work outside the home and do not earn income.

Mothers who stay at home are generally less educated and earn fewer household dollars than mothers who work outside the home. Thus, in the past few decades, the American family has diversified. It has also become more complex, with even greater diversity in family structure and even more astonishing changes in fertility rates. And now we have mothers with a seemingly infinite variety of work lives.

With this data in mind, one must wonder how Aristotle and Kant would view this current trajectory considering their views that principles of reciprocity, interdependence, ethics, and virtue are instilled in a balanced microcosm of a family unit. Will we see a future with fewer of these attributes being present in society at large?

7. SOCIAL MEDIA—AN EVOLVING LANDSCAPE FOR THE FAMILY

"We're living in a culture where everyone is connected,
but no one is connecting."
—Some robot

At a recent dinner, I was in a conversation with other parents, and the conversation came around to social media and this new world that we parent in. One couple said that they were taking the iPhone away from their daughter because of her social media use. This seemed like an odd course of action to me because the reason that we gave the phones in the first place was for safety and also trackability. We get to know where they are. I am all for minimizing screen time, and we won't even know the real effects of this new echelon of children and screens for some time, but there are other ways. For example, you can lock down apps for time-limited access.

This conversation moved my mind to the idea of border security. It is a politically weaponized topic right now in America, and this book is certainly not a platform for politics in any way, but applying the idea of border security to phones is a very interesting topic. All sorts of people are up in arms about supposed border threats, and the reported severity or even the existence of a genuine threat depends on which side of the political aisle you tend to hang out in. One thing is for sure, however, and that is that these borders that are supposed to be in place to protect our children's eyes and minds are wide open, and the threat is palpable. Cyberbullying is one thing, and we will explore that too but let's just consider for one moment the growing epidemic of human trafficking.

The idea that illicit drugs can only be sold once, but a person can be sold all day, every day, has driven an economy in human trafficking unlike anything we've ever seen. Children who are struggling socially or in the home don't know where to turn, so when somebody shows kindness and acceptance, it is embraced enthusiastically. Before you know it, your child is being lured into a dark world of criminal activities that is terrifying.

We used to think that this type of trafficking was rife in other countries, but it is as right at our door. Even seemingly quiet and wholesome towns like Billings, Montana, are experiencing the shocking frequency and scale of this industry. Where there is a hub of highways, we are seeing unprecedented growth in this new threat.

Most people are unaware of the magnitude of human trafficking in America, but law enforcement is increasing defenses daily. The Department Of Justice has created task forces such as ICAC (Internet Crimes Against Children) just to deal with threats such as sextortion. The fact that there is now a word for it is emblematic of the growing concern. Children are lured in by master manipulators using cutting-edge technology to deep-fake identities. Even masquerading as friends of the child using video emulation technology and encouraging the child to take inappropriate photographs. As soon as they have what they want, the extortion begins, and children are asked to pay money to stop the images from being shared with friends, schoolteachers, and even sports coaches or the college where the child intends to go. And they pay. Even if it's small amounts, lunch money, or borrowing from friends, they are so scared of the images being shared that they find a way to keep paying. Some children have paid thousands, and others have committed suicide over the potential exposure. There are entire workforces around the world dedicated to this type of manipulation and extortion, and everyone is a target, not just children.

These open borders and windows or conduits into our children's bedrooms are a palpable threat, and the only possible security is education. Law enforcement state to state is introducing programs into schools to educate children on these threats, but parents need education on this too, or their children are so exposed it is unimaginable.

But let's explore how we got here in such a short time. It seems like only a minute ago, we didn't even have cell phones. Remember stopping in traffic to find a phone booth? The speed at which our generation has experienced change is bewildering.

Since its inception, social media has had an immense impact on nearly every aspect of modern life, including family dynamics. As platforms like Facebook, Twitter, Instagram, and TikTok have become ubiquitous, they have reshaped the ways in which families communicate, bond, and interact with the world. This chapter will explore the multifaceted effects of social media on families, examining both the positive and negative outcomes that have emerged over time.

Early Adoption and the Changing Nature of Communication

When social media first emerged in the early 2000s, it was primarily seen as a tool for connecting people across distances. Families, especially those with members separated by geography, were early adopters, using platforms like Facebook to stay in touch. The ability to share updates, photos, and messages in real time revolutionized long-distance relationships within families.

However, as social media became more integrated into everyday life, it began to alter the nature of communication, even among family members living under the same roof. While in-person conversations traditionally formed the backbone of familial interactions, the rise of messaging apps and online communication led to a shift. Parents and children began communicating through text messages, direct messages, and even comments on each other's social media posts. This shift, though convenient, often reduced the depth and quality of conversations. Face-to-face interactions were sometimes replaced with brief, impersonal exchanges online, leading to a decline in meaningful, in-depth discussions.

The Impact on Family Relationships

As social media continued to evolve, its effects on family relationships became more pronounced. On one hand, these platforms provided new opportunities for bonding. Families could share in each other's lives, even from a distance, and create virtual communities where extended relatives, who might otherwise lose touch, could stay connected.

On the other hand, the omnipresence of social media created new tensions. The advent of social comparison—where people constantly measure their lives against the curated, often idealized versions of others' lives posted online—began to infiltrate family dynamics. This phenomenon did not spare families; parents and children alike began to feel pressure to present their lives in a certain way online, sometimes creating tension when the reality of their home life did not match the image portrayed on social media.

Furthermore, the rise of influencer culture and increasing social media monetization have introduced a new element to family life. Some families have become influencers themselves, sharing intimate details of their lives for public consumption. While this has opened up new financial opportunities, it has also raised concerns about privacy, exploitation, and the blurring of boundaries between public and private life.

Effects on Children and Adolescents

For young people, social media has become a central part of their social lives, with platforms like Instagram, Snapchat, and TikTok dominating their free time. While these platforms offer opportunities for creativity, self-expression, and connection, they also expose children to a range of risks.

Cyberbullying has become a major concern for parents, as social media provides a new avenue for harassment. Although it is a lesser threat than trafficking, it is still a significant influence and can disrupt or even destroy lives. Unlike traditional bullying, which might be confined to the school environment, cyberbullying can follow children into their homes, creating a sense of constant vulnerability. The anonymous nature of some platforms can exacerbate this issue, as bullies feel emboldened by the lack of accountability.

Additionally, social media has been linked to increased anxiety and depression among young people. The pressure to conform to certain standards of beauty, success, and lifestyle—amplified by social media algorithms that promote popular content—can be overwhelming. Parents often find themselves navigating the difficult task of monitoring their children's social media use while respecting their privacy and independence.

Moreover, screen time has become a growing concern. With children spending hours each day on social media, parents are faced with the challenge of setting boundaries and encouraging offline activities. The addictive nature of social media, driven by algorithms designed to maximize engagement, has led to concerns about the long-term effects on attention span, social skills, and overall mental health. Tests have been conducted using MRI where unhealthy brain activity (cognitive decline) reveals itself when engaging on these platforms for extended periods. Extensive studies have been creative for long-term monitoring of these effects, one such platform is ChildrenAndScreens.org, created by the Institute of Digital Media and Child Development.

Parental Influence and Role Modeling

Parents, too, are influenced by social media, and their behavior online can have a profound impact on their children. The rise of "sharenting"—the practice of parents sharing photos and updates about their children on social media—has sparked debates about consent and privacy. While many parents see it as a way to document their children's lives and share milestones with friends and family, others worry about the long-term implications of creating a digital footprint for their children before they are old enough to make informed decisions.

Additionally, parents' own social media habits can influence their children's behavior. Studies have shown that children are likely to model their parents' screen time habits, meaning that if parents are constantly on their phones, their children are more likely to follow suit. This has led to concerns about the impact of social media on family bonding time, with some families finding it difficult to disconnect from their devices and engage in meaningful, offline interactions.

The Role of Social Media in Family Conflict

Social media has also introduced new avenues for conflict within families. Disagreements over screen time, privacy, and appropriate content consumption have become common in households across the world. Parents often struggle to find the right balance between allowing their children the freedom to explore the digital world and protecting them from the risks that social media can pose.

Moreover, social media can sometimes become a platform for family conflicts to spill into the public domain. Arguments that might have previously remained private can now be played out in comment sections or through passive-aggressive posts, leading to embarrassment and further strain on relationships.

The Future of Families and Social Media

As social media continues to evolve, so too will its impact on families. New platforms will emerge, each with its own set of challenges and opportunities, and families will need to adapt to these changes. The growing awareness of the potential negative effects of social media has led to increased efforts to educate both parents and children about responsible usage, digital literacy, and the importance of maintaining a healthy balance between online and offline life.

At the same time, social media is unlikely to disappear from family life. It will remain a powerful connection and communication tool, offering families opportunities to stay close despite physical distances. The challenge moving forward will be to harness the positive aspects of social media while mitigating its negative effects, ensuring that it serves as a tool for strengthening, rather than undermining, family relationships.

* * *

Dr. Vivek Murthy, the US Surgeon General, has recently expressed significant concern about the impact of social media use on children and the associated stress it places on parents. He highlights that excessive social media exposure can be detrimental to children's mental health, leading to issues like anxiety, depression, and poor self-esteem. Dr. Murthy emphasizes that the design of social media platforms often exploits children's vulnerabilities by encouraging excessive screen time and exposure to harmful content.

He also addresses the stress this environment places on parents, who often struggle to monitor and manage their children's social media use in a landscape where technology rapidly evolves and social norms around digital use are still developing. Murthy calls for stronger regulations, better tools for parents, and a collective effort from society to protect children from the potential harms of social media. He advocates for more research into the long-term effects of social media on youth and stresses the importance of fostering open communication within families about the digital world.

Dr. Murthy also shared the importance of exercising social muscles. College dining rooms used to be the loudest place on campus, he noted, but now you'll notice that they are far quieter. Students feel that approaching other children who are using earbuds and engaged with their phones seems like an imposition or interruption so social interaction is discouraged. The less we do it, the less we will want to do it and the less we are skilled at social interaction which moves children and everyone further inward and further engaged in a digital world rather than healthy social interaction.

People are becoming less happy, and happiness has a direct correlation with health. Dr. Murthy, who has two children himself, says that parents are overwhelmed and burned out with the dizzying pace of the world and calls for a culture shift in support of parents and caregivers.

While working on the youth health crisis, he found that 48%, nearly half of parents, are saying that on most days, they are completely overwhelmed by their stress. That is an extraordinary number that should alarm all of us.

He also found that parents are struggling with loneliness at levels that are higher than other adults. Particularly when you look at single parents, more than 75% of them are saying they're struggling with loneliness. Now, stress and loneliness together form a tough combination that can take a real toll on the mental health and well-being of parents.

There are a few things that have contributed. Parents for generations have worried about kids' safety. They've worried about their education and a whole host of things related to children, including how to manage the difficult teenage years. But there are some new factors that parents are dealing with today that our parents and grandparents didn't have to contend with, like how to manage social media and technology and phones in your kid's life, how to contend with a loneliness epidemic in a youth mental health crisis that's taking a profound toll on millions of kids, and also how to deal with issues like gun violence, which is now a powerful source of fear for parents and kids. Keep in mind, more than half of kids are worried now about a shooting taking place in their school. You put all of this together with one other critical factor and that's this intensified culture of comparison that we're all living in that's fed and potentiated by social media, the online environment where parents are looking around them and comparing themselves to sometimes hundreds of other parents, some of whom they know, some of whom they don't know but they often come away feeling worse about themselves and like they're falling short as parents.

This is the same thing that kids are going through on social media in that regard, this comparison culture of everybody's life on social media seems so much better than your own life. Kids feel that way and it's interesting to hear that so many parents feel that way.

But what's the answer to this? Changing behaviors is very difficult and we are in uncharted waters. It would seem that our only option is communication. Talking with children and with each other about these very real dangers is the most powerful thing we can do to help reduce the threats and move back toward healthier, happier, and safer environments.

Conclusion

While it has undoubtedly created new opportunities for connection and communication, it has also introduced considerable new challenges and risks for us to consider and try to solve. As families continue to navigate this evolving digital landscape, the key will be finding ways to balance the benefits of social media with the need to protect family bonds, privacy, and mental health. Our best defense is to share knowledge and communicate with our children and each other about this perilous new landscape in which we find ourselves. A robust topic for the new Secretary of The American Family, which we will explore in the epilogue.

8. THE EVOLUTION OF THE AMERICAN COMMUNITY

"Family is not an important thing. It's everything. But it thrives best when surrounded by a supportive community."
— Adaptation of Michael J. Fox

Great engineering with poor prejudicial motives does not a great country make.

The A train from the Bronx to the Atlantic Ocean is a standout anomaly that put Coney Island in everyone's backyard, but many worked against infrastructure like this.

To understand the state of families in America we must include the exploration of how communities have evolved. We are still a young country with a long way to go, but if we are not acutely aware of what we have done to get where we are, we are not really in charge of our own path forward. As we all know, without carefully studying history, we will repeat it again and again.

Whether it be well-intentioned, misinformed, or simply misled, mistakes have been made. Let's begin with Robert Moses, for example. Often hailed as the visionary behind some of the most ambitious infrastructure projects in New York City, Robert Moses remains a controversial figure in urban planning for good reason. His celebrated work and its undoubted impact on our lives cannot be disentangled from the divisive and damaging choices he made, the policies he pushed, and the kind of society he helped make a reality. One of the most notorious aspects of his highway plans—and a clear indication of his not-so-hidden agenda—was the design of overpasses that were low enough to block buses from going onto the suburban-style parkways he built.

The routes Moses built to Jones Beach, a well-frequented leisure destination, were often decorated with low bridges, which were constructed with such intent and care that their heights successfully prohibited not just large vehicles but effectively any vehicles whose drivers might be capable of paying tolls, from passing beneath them.

This way, certain vehicles, and consequently those who must travel in them, were unable to visit Jones Beach conveniently. Why not just make the bridges low enough that the only vehicles that could get through would be those who Moses and team deemed worthy to have access to the beach?

The exclusionary approach taken by Robert Moses and his cohorts exemplified the way urban planning was moving in the mid-20th century—a direction that blatantly ignored the needs and the voices of the less privileged. Not merely pedestrians in the situation but also critics of the plan have charged that Moses's choices were about more than just the efficient movement of people; they say they were also about keeping certain kinds of people in certain kinds of places and, consequently, about maintaining the status quo. Instead of finding ways to integrate communities and connect the various parts of a city, Moses built highways that made the divisions sharper and more intense, in the process imparting a set of intersectional critiques regarding race, class, and the appearances of urban development in the American landscape.

Now, let's travel backward in time to post-World War II. Suburban development and the efforts to maintain racial and cultural segregation were being very carefully managed. The newly formed suburban neighborhoods, which are often idealized as the American Dream, were formed through many means, including covenants that restricted homeowners to certain racial and ethnic groups. These practices not only maintained existing social hierarchies but formed the basis for living in the suburbs and not seeing any minority group since even the appearance of minorities was prohibited in many ways. The Federal Housing Administration (FHA) was a key player in developing these discriminatory practices. It inscribed them into law when it endorsed and financed projects that followed them. The FHA funneled more than $120 billion into the construction of homes and the making of communities over the span of 40 years. Loans and insurance from the FHA went strongly into communities that were defined as "predominantly white." For all intents and purposes, this was behavior equal to white supremacy. The FHA was subsidizing builders who were mass-producing entire subdivisions for whites with the explicit requirement that none of the homes be sold to African Americans. the local, state, and federal housing policies that mandated segregation. The Federal Housing Administration—established in 1934—furthered the segregation efforts by refusing to insure mortgages in and near African American neighborhoods — a practice known as "redlining."

These suburbs were molded by designs that kept segregation in place. The appearance of highways and the routing of public transportation were planned to keep minority enclaves away from affluent suburban areas. As a result, the suburban landscape became a mirror of societal values, reflecting the ideal of a calm, homogeneous community and masking the mechanisms of exclusion and inequality that made it so. In hindsight, the subdivision of America is not just a matter of mapping but a profoundly racial development that continues to shape social interaction and dynamics to this day.

Obviously, these practices drastically affect the American Family. Without cultural and racial diversity, further segregation is a charted course and a foregone conclusion.

9. NAVIGATING THE INTERSECTION OF RELIGION AND PARENTING

"Children are great imitators, so give them something great to imitate. Let your faith be the guide in teaching them love, kindness, and humility."
—Dr. Jerry Cammarata

As we consider the future of the American family, one of the most significant factors influencing its evolution is the role of religion. The United States has always been a diverse mosaic of religious beliefs, each contributing to the fabric of society in unique ways. However, this diversity also presents challenges, particularly when religious ideologies become so dominant that they threaten to overshadow individual parenting choices and the broader values of freedom and inclusivity that define America.

Religious extremism, regardless of its origin, can stifle the individuality that is essential to effective parenting. When any single religious ideology becomes so entrenched that it dictates every aspect of family life, the ability of parents to make informed, thoughtful decisions for their children diminishes. Parenting should be a dynamic process, one that adapts to the changing world, informed by a wide range of experiences and perspectives. It must never be reduced to dogma but should instead be an expression of what works best for each family, rooted in a broader understanding of the world.

The American family thrives when it is allowed to reflect the diversity of our nation. Whether through traditional religious practices or more contemporary forms of spirituality, parents must have the freedom to choose how they wish to raise their children. This choice is essential not only for the development of well-rounded individuals but also for maintaining the core spirit of America—a spirit that values freedom, diversity, and the right to self-determination.

However, when religion is wielded as a political tool, it can become divisive. The more that certain religious groups seek to align themselves with political power, the more likely they are to face rejection from broader society. The principle of separating church and state is not just about keeping religion out of government; it's also about ensuring that government does not interfere with religious practices. This separation is crucial for preserving the integrity of both institutions and for allowing families the space to cultivate their own values without undue external pressure.

Education is another area where the intersection of religion and family life becomes particularly complex. In a nation where parents sometimes feel compelled to send their children to parochial schools to ensure a quality education, the question arises: shouldn't all schools—public, private, and parochial—offer equally high standards of education? The need for such choices often reflects broader systemic issues, and addressing these could help alleviate the pressure on families to conform to particular religious practices simply for the sake of their children's education.

The impact of religion on child development is a topic of ongoing debate. Some studies suggest that religious households can foster social and psychological skills, while others indicate that rigid religious beliefs can hinder academic performance and lead to more authoritarian parenting styles. The challenge for the American family, then, is to navigate these complex dynamics in a way that supports the healthy development of children while respecting the diverse religious and spiritual landscapes in which they are raised.

As we move forward, it's essential to recognize that the American family is not a monolith. It is a reflection of our nation's rich tapestry of beliefs, practices, and values. To ensure that the American family can build a healthy future, we must embrace this diversity, allowing parents the freedom to choose how they wish to raise their children while safeguarding the rights of all to practice—or not practice—religion as they see fit. Only by maintaining this balance can we hope to nurture the next generation in a way that honors both our individual freedoms and our collective identity as a nation.

In summary, families must feel comfortable and be respected for the manner in which they wish to practice their religious beliefs and work to keep those beliefs alive through their future generations. Every family deserves that choice.

10. THE HAVE AND HAVE NOTS—GETTING BIGGER AND FURTHER APART

"The rich get richer, and the poor get poorer—not because of fate, but because of the systems we build and sustain."
— Joseph E. Stiglitz

The American Dream has long been held as a beacon of hope, a promise that hard work and perseverance will lead to prosperity and success. For generations, families across the United States have aspired to build better lives for themselves and their children, fueled by the belief that opportunity is within reach for those who strive for it. However, as the 21st century unfolds, a stark and troubling reality has emerged: the socioeconomic divide in America is widening at an alarming rate, with profound implications for the future of the American family. This growing chasm between the "haves" and the "have-nots" threatens not only the fabric of individual lives but also the very cohesion of society as a whole.

The Expanding Wealth Gap

The numbers tell a sobering story. Over the past few decades, income inequality in the United States has reached levels not seen since the Gilded Age. The top 1% of Americans now hold more wealth than the entire bottom 90% combined. The middle class, once the backbone of the American economy and the bedrock of family stability, is shrinking as the cost of living outpaces wage growth. In cities across the country, from New York to San Francisco, the divide between affluent neighborhoods and impoverished ones is stark, with the former boasting luxury condos and high-end retail, while the latter struggle with underfunded schools, food deserts, and crumbling infrastructure.

This wealth disparity is not just about dollars and cents; it is about the opportunities and life chances that are available to different segments of the population. For those at the top of the economic ladder, the future seems bright—access to the best schools, healthcare, and social networks ensures that their children will likely inherit not only wealth but also the means to generate more of it. On the other hand, for those at the bottom, the obstacles to upward mobility are becoming increasingly insurmountable. The lack of access to quality education, affordable healthcare, and stable employment traps many families in a cycle of poverty that is difficult, if not impossible, to escape.

The Impact on Family Structure

As the economic divide grows, it is reshaping the structure and stability of American families. In wealthier communities, marriage rates remain relatively high, and families often have the resources to support both parents being present and involved in their children's lives. These families can afford quality childcare, extracurricular activities, and the luxury of time—time to nurture relationships, support children's education, and build a strong family unit.

In contrast, in economically disadvantaged communities, the picture is much bleaker. Marriage rates have declined sharply among low-income Americans, driven by financial insecurity and the stresses associated with poverty. Single-parent households are far more common, and these parents often juggle multiple jobs with little time or resources to devote to their children. The lack of financial stability makes it difficult to maintain a cohesive family unit, leading to higher rates of divorce, family estrangement, and a host of other social challenges.

Children growing up in these environments face an uphill battle. The stress of economic hardship can lead to a range of adverse outcomes, from poor academic performance to mental health issues. Without the safety net of a stable family structure, these children are more likely to drop out of school, become involved in criminal activity, or face teenage pregnancy. The cycle of poverty, once started, becomes difficult to break, perpetuating the divide between the haves and have-nots.

Education: The Great Divider

Education has long been touted as the great equalizer in American society—the key to breaking the cycle of poverty and achieving upward mobility. Yet, the reality in today's America is that education is increasingly becoming a divider, rather than a unifier. Public schools in affluent areas are often well-funded, with small class sizes, experienced teachers, and a wealth of resources. In these schools, students have access to advanced placement courses, state-of-the-art technology, and extracurricular activities that enhance their college applications and prepare them for successful careers.

Meanwhile, schools in low-income areas are frequently underfunded and overcrowded, with outdated textbooks, limited technology, and fewer opportunities for students to excel. Teachers in these schools are often underpaid and overworked, struggling to provide a quality education under challenging circumstances. The achievement gap between wealthy and poor students is widening, with children from affluent families far more likely to attend college and secure high-paying jobs.

The implications of this educational divide are profound. Without access to quality education, children from low-income families are at a significant disadvantage in the job market. As the economy becomes increasingly reliant on technology and specialized skills, the lack of a solid educational foundation can be a lifelong barrier to economic success. The result is a self-perpetuating cycle where the wealthy can continue to invest in their children's future, while the poor are left to struggle with limited opportunities. We will explore education in greater depth in the next chapter to uncover threats and opportunities.

The Social and Political Consequences

The widening socioeconomic divide is not just a personal or familial issue—it has broader social and political implications that threaten the stability of the nation. As the gap between the wealthy and the poor grows, so too does social unrest. Feelings of disenfranchisement, resentment, and anger are simmering beneath the surface of American society, manifesting in increased political polarization, social movements, and, at times, violent confrontations.

The erosion of the middle class has also led to a loss of trust in institutions, including the government, media, and education system. Many Americans feel that the system is rigged in favor of the wealthy and powerful, leading to a rise in populism and a rejection of traditional political norms. This distrust undermines the social contract that binds communities together and threatens the democratic principles upon which the country was founded.

The Dangerous Trajectory

If current trends continue, the socioeconomic divide in America will only deepen, with dire consequences for the future of the American family. The American Dream, once a unifying force that offered hope and aspiration to all, is at risk of becoming a relic of the past, accessible only to a privileged few. The country is on a dangerous trajectory, one where the rich get richer, the poor get poorer, and the middle-class fades into obscurity.

To reverse this trend, bold and innovative solutions are required. Policies that address income inequality, provide access to quality education and healthcare, and support family stability must be prioritized. The future of the American family—and indeed the future of the nation—depends on our ability to bridge the growing divide and create a society where opportunity is truly available to all.

In the end, the question we must ask ourselves is not just what kind of country we want to live in, but what kind of country we want to leave to our children and their families. The choices we make today will determine whether the American family thrives and once again becomes the center piece of our society, or whether the divide between the haves and have-nots continues to grow, pulling us further apart with each passing generation.

11. THE EDUCATION CRISIS

"Education is the most powerful weapon which you can use to change the world. Yet, when denied or neglected, it becomes the greatest inequality of our time."
— Nelson Mandela

Despite charging more for education and creating a lifelong debt burden for our children, America's performance in global education generally ranks as average to slightly above average compared to other developed nations. Here's an overview of where the United States stands and its main competitors in global education rankings:

Key Global Education Rankings

1. **Program for International Student Assessment (PISA)**
   - PISA is conducted by the Organization for Economic Co-operation and Development (OECD) every three years and assesses 15-year-olds' abilities in reading, mathematics, and science.
   - **2022 Rankings:**
     - Reading: The United States ranked 13th.
     - Mathematics: The United States ranked 37th.
     - Science: The United States ranked 18th.
   - **Competitors:** Countries like China (specifically the regions of Beijing, Shanghai, Jiangsu, and Zhejiang), Singapore, Japan, South Korea, Finland, and Canada often top the PISA rankings in all subjects, particularly in math and science.
2. **Trends in International Mathematics and Science Study (TIMSS)**
   - TIMSS is conducted every four years by the International Association for the Evaluation of Educational Achievement (IEA) and measures students' achievements in mathematics and science at the 4th- and 8th-grade levels.
   - **2020 Rankings (latest available):**
     - 4th Grade Mathematics: The United States ranked 15th.

- 8th Grade Mathematics: The United States ranked 11th.
- 4th Grade Science: The United States ranked 9th.
- 8th Grade Science: The United States ranked 10th.
- Competitors: Countries like Singapore, South Korea, Hong Kong, Taiwan, and Japan consistently rank higher in both math and science.

3. **Progress in International Reading Literacy Study (PIRLS)**
   - PIRLS measures reading comprehension of 4th-grade students around the world.
   - 2021 Rankings (latest available):
     The United States ranked 15th out of 57 participating countries.
   - Competitors: Countries such as Singapore, Russia, Hong Kong, Ireland, and Finland perform better than the United States in reading literacy at the primary school level.

4. **World Economic Forum (Global Competitiveness Report)**
   The Global Competitiveness Report ranks countries based on their overall competitiveness, which includes education as one of its key pillars. In the 2020 report, the United States ranked 20th for its education system's quality, with countries like Switzerland, Finland, and Singapore consistently performing better. The usual top performers are European nations (e.g., Switzerland, Finland, and the Netherlands) and Asian countries (e.g., Singapore, South Korea, and Japan).

5. **Education Index—United Nations Development Program (UNDP)**
   - The Education Index, part of the Human Development Index (HDI), measures a country's education level based on the average years of schooling for adults and expected years of schooling for children.
   - The United States typically ranks within the top 15 globally, but countries like Norway, Germany, and Australia often rank higher.
   - Competitors: High-ranking countries often include Norway, Switzerland, Australia, and Ireland, which have strong overall education systems.

Strengths and Weaknesses of US Education

Strengths

- **Higher Education:** The United States is a global leader in higher education. American universities dominate international rankings (e.g., QS World University Rankings, Times Higher Education), with institutions like Harvard, MIT, and Stanford frequently taking top spots.

- **Innovation and Research:** The United States excels in fostering innovation, research, and STEM (science, technology, engineering, and mathematics) fields in higher education.
- **Diversity of Curriculum:** The US education system offers a broad curriculum with opportunities for specialization, particularly in higher education.

Weaknesses

- **K-12 System:** The US K-12 education system has notable disparities, particularly between different states and socioeconomic groups, resulting in a wide variance in student outcomes.
- **Mathematics and Science:** The United States lags behind many developed countries in math and science education, as reflected in PISA and TIMSS rankings.
- **Inequality:** Socioeconomic inequality affects access to quality education, and underfunded public schools in certain areas struggle to provide the same level of education as those in wealthier districts.

Competitors in Global Education

The United States faces competition from several countries that consistently outperform in global education rankings:

1. **East Asia:**
   China (particularly Shanghai and Beijing regions), Singapore, South Korea, Japan, and Hong Kong consistently rank at the top in mathematics, science, and reading. These countries have strong K-12 education systems with a focus on rigorous curriculum and high standards for academic achievement.
2. **Scandinavia and Northern Europe:**
   Finland, Norway, and Estonia are known for their high-quality education systems, emphasizing equality, teacher professionalism, and innovative teaching methods. Finland, in particular, has long been a model for education reform.
3. **Canada:**
   Canada consistently ranks among the top-performing countries, particularly in reading and science. Its decentralized education system emphasizes equity and has strong outcomes across different provinces.

4. **Western Europe:**
   Netherlands, Switzerland, Germany, and Ireland also perform well in global education rankings, particularly in reading and science literacy. These countries benefit from well-funded public education systems and strong vocational training programs.

In summary, the United States performs well in higher education but faces challenges in K-12 education, particularly in math and science. Competitors such as Singapore, Finland, South Korea, Japan, and Canada consistently rank higher in various global education metrics. The United States could improve by addressing inequality, reforming STEM education, and adopting successful strategies from top-performing nations.

* * *

The drop in US education standards is a compounded problem, affected by many different things. Experts point to different prime movers, but here are a couple that appear frequently. One is inequality, a long-term, systemic issue in our country. "U.S. public education suffers from the same kind of resource inequality found throughout American society," says Susan Ohanian, an educator who is extremely well read in both the history of public education and current conditions. "The reason some kids are not learning is that those kids and their schools do not have as many resources as the kids who are learning."

Public schools in the United States receive their primary funding from local property taxes. This means that your wealth or poverty, and the accompanying disparities in property values, determine—for the most part—how well your public school serves you and your children. The next layer of equality (or inequality) is determined by how good or bad the state you live in has been at maintaining a funding balance between poor and rich districts. Since the federal government is not half as generous as it should be, this funding mechanism determines in large part how much opportunity there is for you and your children. With a focus on education at a federal level, new directions could be forged.

Teachers in the United States are often undercompensated and overworked which leads inevitably to an excessive number of them leaving the profession and a greater difficulty in attracting and keeping qualified people.

This is occurring at a disastrously fast rate in our most difficult-to-staff schools, where teachers by any reasonable measure should be given far more help.

The US education system has become fixated on standardized testing as the sole measure of student and school success. The tests may not be very meaningful in themselves, as the kind of knowledge that can be demonstrated on a test is often shallow and not very useful in the real world. The tests may not even measure what they claim to measure. Still, they are taken very seriously, and a lot of teaching goes on not just to the test but also in a way that narrows the curriculum so that almost everything taught is somehow related to the test. This all contributes to the stifling of innovation in teaching and learning.

Certain features of the American curriculum have not kept up with the changing demands of the modern world. For example, there is often an insufficient emphasis on STEM education, digital literacy, and, especially, critical thinking. These are the very areas in which most members of society need to be functioning at a high level if society is to succeed. The old standbys of rote learning and passive reception of information simply do not engage students or prepare them for the real challenges of modern life.

Early childhood education is absolutely critical to cognitive and social development. The research is so strong that it has become virtually irrefutable. If we want to give our kids a shot at competing on a level playing field, we've got to make sure that they can go to preschool. But too many kids can't. And especially too many kids from low-income families. That's a double inequality that's compounded over the years by the sorts of harmful educational outcomes that early disparities tend to generate.

The home environment and family engagement in education play a crucial role in a child's academic success. They are the first educators a child has and the primary influence on a child's estimation of the importance of education. However, there are many constraints that limit the ability of families to be fully engaged in their child's education, especially in low-income communities. Some communities might even have a negative culture around education that serves to further limit family engagement and the positive attitudes of children toward education.

The US education system is highly decentralized, with significant variations in standards, curriculum, and accountability measures from state to state. This decentralization produces a very uneven "playing field." While some states have adopted high-quality standards and assessments and have made serious efforts to hold all schools accountable, other states have pocketed the gains and have not changed their own low practices. These inconsistencies in policy and the absence of national standards must change if we are to put American education back on course.

As if we were not already challenged enough, the proliferation of digital technology and social media has brought new diversions that detract from student concentration on their studies. These increased diversions are directly correlated with the decline of the attention span and the rise of the poor academic performance of today's youth.

The kinds of problems students face are diverse and complex, pushing many of them to the brink. They involve social and behavioral dimensions—like bullying, for instance—that don't speak directly to the issue of the quality of a student's brain, but they nonetheless exert powerful influences on the learning and performance that a student is capable of. Then there are the direct and powerful influences exuded by ill mental health. At the very time when a student is attempting to master the many demands of one's educational lot, their brain is simply not functioning up to par because it's under the duress of a not-yet resolved mental health issue—and an awful lot of students are walking around with mental health issues—or because a student under the crown of a mental health problem is simply not thriving.

The drop in US education quality is not due to a single cause. It demands a multifaceted solution. Funding a new direction is not really the issue, the problem is lack of a clear direction. So many attempts in so many directions will leave us dazed and confused. A consolidated, comprehensive plan is required to overhaul education. Taking the examples set by high-performing institutions and creating a set of principles on which to build a new foundation for education that is accessible to all with minimal cost would be a very good start. We must create—or re-create—an environment in which learning is seen as valuable. Putting our children into debt for their education is the worst possible message we can give them. So many countries—mostly high performing ones—are providing education at every level for free or nearly free that it is very hard to argue against the model. Student debt, like privatized heath care was created for profit, driven by greed and it must end if we are to change the trajectory of our youth and their education.

There is a powerful and terrifying word to describe the effects of war on schools in war zones. It is scholasticide. Often used interchangeably with the terms educide and epistemicide, and usually refers to the intended mass destruction of education in a specific place. Educide has been used to describe the mass destruction in the Iraq War and the Israeli invasion of Gaza, for example. But I believe it also applies here in the context of our American children. We have a responsibility to our children to lift the level of education to compete with the world, or we are not the superpower we delusionally dreamed we were. If we do not reverse the damage we have done and put measures in place to fix education from the ground up, I would consider this scholasticide.

Now, on to higher learning. At the time of this writing, a medical school in New York is introducing a radically innovative, although, in retrospect, completely commonsensical, framework for medical students. As we reengineer graduate programs on a continuous basis and get students into practice early, the concept of reinventing our national public education system is absent of making education relevant. But what New York Medical College is doing is transformative. The institution's website outlines the overview:

> The School of Medicine (SOM) Class of 2026 will be the first class to experience the new medical education curriculum launched this year at New York Medical College (NYMC). The new curriculum, which was developed by a broad representation of SOM administration, faculty, and students, integrates basic science and clinical course content during the first eighteen months of medical education while also allowing students to enter clerkships much earlier in their education.

> "In the old curriculum, the discipline-based courses, such as histology, anatomy, pathophysiology, and pharmacology, were taught separately. Now we've completely integrated those courses, so they no longer exist in isolation," said Pamela Ludmer, M.D., M.S., associate dean for curriculum integration. "The first new course, Fundamental Processes of Life, incorporates the basic foundational principles from some of these different disciplines, as well as biochemistry, ethics and patient care. This is extremely important because as physicians, we don't think of pharmacology, anatomy and histology, for example, separately from patient care. We look at the patient as a whole person and think of everything as being connected. And so, we want to teach our medical students how to integrate this knowledge together from the start."

Later in the first year of the new curriculum, students take an introduction to systems course, which bridges the content from the fundamental processes course, introduces concepts that will be applied throughout the remaining courses and further integrates basic science with patient care and health systems science principles.

"The focus is to create courses that are not siloed but are integrated organ systems-based, including brain and behavior, cardiorespiratory, renal/reproductive/endocrine and gastroenterology/dermatology/rheumatology," said Dr. Ludmer. "Another important area of focus is health system science, in which we teach students concepts that allow them to function in a very complex healthcare system—patient safety, quality improvement, high-value care, leadership, and teamwork. And this is something we've been incorporating not just into this new curriculum but for all our classes of students."

"One of the most gratifying aspects of the development of this new curriculum has been how hard the faculty have worked," said Dr. Ludmer. "Putting this all together was much more than just moving established lectures to different places in the curriculum. It required a completely new approach to teaching with basic science faculty and clinicians working together to ensure the coursework is fully integrated."

In addition, as part of the new curriculum, students will also enter clerkships three months earlier – in April of their second year of medical education—allowing them more time to solidify their clinical skills, complete scholarly projects, and prepare for residency.

"Previously, students were starting their advanced clerkships at the start of the fourth year in July, giving them only a few months before they needed to make their choice of specialty decisions and begin applying to residency programs," said Dr. Ludmer.

This is a beautiful example of positive innovation with a clear and concise outcome focus. It is highly executable and immediately measurable. A holistic approach to medicine is long overdue, and the idea of getting real-world experience far earlier is a must-have in my view. Yes, basic info must still be learned, but to learn it in the morning and then in the afternoon, attend application classes—or on a rotational schedule, go to businesses where applications are seen, gives rise to curiosity and provides irreplaceable field experience. A dramatic upgrade to our education system.

*Solutions:

1: Repurposing college debt. Just imagine if student loans became start-up capital to fund innovative ideas led by the student who is responsible for the loan. Now, there is a level of education that can only be obtained by doing it. Within the framework of a mentoring organization to guide and promote success, startups could thrive and provide at-work education heretofore unseen.

The idea of turning the system upside down and starting work immediately out of high school while being evaluated for your degree by what you do at work is a framework that is not being given enough attention. It would better prepare students for the real world immediately, provide income instead of debt, and give a sense of fulfillment that students don't experience until years after leaving college and joining the workforce. Working at a law firm while studying the law is so much more powerful than the classroom because your knowledge is put into practice every day. Admittedly, we can't have medical students performing surgery without the foundational knowledge and experience which is why the residency is an integral part of becoming a doctor but almost any other vocation could be best learned while working for your degree.

Philanthropy. Teaching children giving is a platform for bonding in any family.

This is important for several key reasons that contribute to their development as compassionate, socially responsible individuals:

Philanthropy helps children understand the needs of others and develop empathy. By learning to care about the welfare of people in their community or the world at large, children become more sensitive to the challenges faced by others.

Engaging in charitable activities teaches children about social issues such as poverty, inequality, and environmental sustainability. This **social awareness** helps them grow into informed and responsible citizens who are more likely to contribute to **positive societal changes.**

When children participate in philanthropic activities, they often gain perspective on their own lives. This can foster a sense of **gratitude** for what they have, leading to a more positive attitude and less entitlement.

Speaking of entitlement. No, the world doesn't owe you. It doesn't owe you success, applause, or a shortcut to the life you've dreamed of. Yet, more and more, entitlement seems to be taking hold. When it does, effort feels optional. Why strive for excellence if you believe you deserve the reward regardless, right? Wrong. Life doesn't work that way.

The most inspiring stories are of people who earned their place—who rolled up their sleeves, made sacrifices, and showed up with grit. Entitlement short-circuits this process. It whispers lies like, "You shouldn't have to wait," or, "You're too good for this," creating a false sense of superiority that attracts the opposite of what you are trying to accomplish.

As an example, I had a call the other evening with a woman who wanted us to turn her idea into a film. I asked if she had a script or a treatment? "No. What's a treatment? Why do I need those things?" she asked. "That's your job. I give you the idea, and you make it happen."

Seeing that she didn't understand how it worked, I explained that if she would like her idea developed, she would have to pay our writers to create a script and treatment. "I don't have the money for that." There was a pause, and then she continued, "You have to tell my story. The world needs to know what happened to me." Not wanting to dismiss her, I suggested she write the script or find a collaborator willing to work for free. I then offered for her to pitch us again once she had a proper script or treatment available. In a huff, she scolded, "No thanks, I don't need you if I have to go out and do those things myself." "Fair enough," I replied kindly. "Ciao, ciao."

Unless you're willing to pay someone for their talent, expecting them to make your dreams come true is unrealistic. Whether in friendships, careers, or partnerships, people gravitate toward those who are willing to put in the work. Walking through the world with an air of entitlement doesn't inspire others to help you; it alienates you. It doesn't connect; it repels. Why? Because the world doesn't owe you a thing. However, there is one person who owes you everything, and that person is you. You owe it to yourself to discover what you're made of, to pour your blood, sweat, and tears into something, and to see it through to completion. When you do, others will want to join you. With that comes the ultimate reward: achievement—an empowering reminder that what you accomplish is earned by your hand, not handed to you.

After all, as with anything worthwhile in life, if you want a stage upon which to rise to your greatest potential, you must be willing to build it.

Teaching philanthropy has the ability to help children realize they have the power to make a difference, no matter their age or means. By engaging in charitable actions, children learn about **responsibility and leadership**, setting them up for future roles in community service or advocacy. Being a giver, not a taker. Not entitled

Children who learn about giving from an early age are more likely to continue philanthropic activities into adulthood and adopt lifelong giving. Early exposure to charitable work can shape their values, making them more inclined to give back as they grow older.

Involving children in family philanthropy or community service projects can **deepen family connections**. It provides an opportunity for shared experiences that reinforce family values and traditions around helping others.

When children engage in philanthropy, they often **think critically** about how to address social issues. Whether through organizing fundraisers, volunteering, or **thinking creatively** about how to solve problems, philanthropy encourages critical thinking and innovation.

By learning about philanthropy, children not only become more compassionate and responsible individuals but also gain valuable skills that can positively impact their communities and the world.

12. THE FOOD CRISIS

"We know that a peaceful world cannot exist when one-third of humanity is well-fed, and two-thirds go hungry."
— Jimmy Carter

While nutrient-rich foods are readily available in the United States, a significant portion of the population consumes a diet that is high in processed, calorie-dense, and nutrient-poor foods. The nutritional value of food in America can be high when individuals focus on whole, minimally processed foods, but the overall dietary pattern tends to fall short of nutritional recommendations for optimal health.

The American diet often includes a large amount of ultra-processed foods, which tend to be high in added sugars, unhealthy fats, sodium, and artificial ingredients, but low in essential nutrients like vitamins, minerals, and fiber. These foods are linked to higher rates of obesity, heart disease, diabetes, and other health issues.

The prevalence of fast food, which is typically calorie-dense but nutrient-poor, further diminishes the overall nutritional quality of the average American diet. Fast food is often rich in unhealthy fats and refined carbohydrates but low in fiber, vitamins, and minerals.

On the positive side, fruits and vegetables available in the United States are diverse and nutrient-dense. However, Americans generally do not consume enough of these foods. According to studies, only a small percentage of adults meet the recommended intake for fruits and vegetables, which are vital sources of vitamins, minerals, and antioxidants.

Some American foods, like cereals and dairy products, are fortified with essential nutrients such as vitamin D, calcium, and iron. Fortification has helped combat certain nutrient deficiencies, but it does not offset the health concerns tied to processed foods.

In recent years, there has been an increasing demand for organic, minimally processed, and locally sourced foods. These tend to be more nutrient-dense, with fewer artificial additives and preservatives, contributing to better overall nutritional value when included in the diet but there is also a disparity in food access. People living in "food deserts" (areas with limited access to affordable and nutritious food) may rely more on convenience stores and fast food, where the nutritional quality of available food is lower compared to supermarkets that offer fresh produce.

High fructose corn syrup (HFCS) has definitely played a major role in the decline of American health. It's been one of those sneaky ingredients that's ended up in a lot of our foods, from sodas and candy to bread and ketchup, and it's had some serious effects on both food and consumers.

HFCS is a super sweet, cheap sugar substitute made from corn (which we have plenty of here in the United States due to government subsidies on corn). It became a go-to ingredient for food manufacturers in the late 20th century because it was way cheaper than cane sugar. But there's a catch, and it's not great news for our health.

HFCS made everything sweeter. It is sweeter than regular sugar, so it's used to make everything taste extra sugary, even things that don't need to be that sweet. I have friends that have moved from other countries that have mentioned the first time they tried bread here that it was more like dessert than the bread they were used to in Australia or the United Kingdom. That is most likely the HFCS.

HFCS is super shelf-stable, which means food companies could pump it into their products to make them last longer. Great for profits, not so great for health. This helped fuel the rise of ultra-processed foods—the kind that are super tasty but not exactly nutrient-rich.

One of the biggest concerns with HFCS is its link to obesity. With so many foods loaded with this sweetener, Americans have been consuming way more calories than they realize, leading to weight gain. HFCS is often blamed for fueling the obesity epidemic that really took off in the late 20th century.

It's not just about weight, though—HFCS has also been linked to other health issues, like type 2 diabetes, heart disease, and liver problems. Studies have shown that fructose (the "F" in HFCS) is metabolized differently than glucose and can lead to fat buildup in the liver, which is definitely not ideal.

Thanks to HFCS, we've somewhat trained our taste buds to crave sweeter and sweeter things. It's like our palates got used to this higher level of sweetness, making it harder to enjoy naturally sweet foods like fruits.

HFCS snuck into American food and made everything a little sweeter, a little more processed, and a lot less healthy. It's been a major contributor to the rise of obesity and other health issues in the United States, and even though people are becoming more aware of it now, it's still lurking in a lot of our favorite foods. The fact that we have to be so diligent just to make sure we are not being poisoned means our societal systems have failed us in this regard.

HFCS has been the unwanted guest at the party who brought dessert and never left. This decline in health most certainly contributes to disorders like depression and, no doubt, many others. Some research even suggests that the overconsumption of HFCS and other sugars may stimulate reward pathways in the brain, leading to increased cravings and patterns of overconsumption, which can mimic addiction. All these things affect our families profoundly. So, where did this all start?

The decline in the quality of food in America can be traced to several key historical shifts: Industrialization of Agriculture (Mid-20th Century): After World War II, advancements in agricultural technology led to the industrialization of farming. This meant the introduction of synthetic fertilizers, pesticides, and large-scale monoculture crops, which contributed to a loss of biodiversity and soil health. While food production increased, the nutritional quality of crops declined as farmers prioritized high yields and profit margins over quality and variety. The post-war period saw a boom in processed foods as companies like Kraft, General Mills, and Nestlé began producing convenient, mass-market products. These foods were often laden with preservatives, artificial flavors, and high amounts of sugar, salt, and fats. While they were marketed as time-savers for busy families, their overconsumption led to a decline in dietary quality, with fresh, whole foods being replaced by packaged alternatives.

Fast food chains like McDonald's, Burger King, and KFC expanded rapidly during the 1970s and 1980s. The emphasis on cheap, quick meals led to the widespread consumption of highly processed, calorie-dense, nutrient-poor foods. Fast food meals became a staple for many Americans, further eroding traditional, home-cooked meals.

US government policies, such as the Farm Bill, subsidized the production of commodity crops like corn, soybeans, and wheat. These crops were used to produce high-fructose corn syrup, refined oils, and other ingredients commonly found in processed foods. As a result, unhealthy, processed foods became cheaper and more accessible than fruits, vegetables, and whole grains. These factors combined over decades, leading to the current state of American food, where highly processed, nutrient-poor options dominate many diets. However, there has been a growing movement toward healthier, organic, and local food in recent years as awareness of these issues has increased.

Then we have wheat, a staple in diets for thousands of years. Modern wheat breeding techniques, such as hybridization, have been ongoing since the early 20th century, with major changes taking place during the 1950s and 1960s, especially during the "Green Revolution."

New varieties of wheat were developed to increase yields, resist diseases, and adapt to different climates. Modern wheat has higher gluten content and more refined starch than its older counterparts, making it easier to bake with but potentially more difficult for some people to digest. Some experts believe that the selective breeding of wheat, particularly for higher gluten content, may be a factor contributing to the increasing number of people experiencing gluten sensitivity or intolerance. Gluten, a protein found in wheat, has been linked to conditions like celiac disease, non-celiac gluten sensitivity, and irritable bowel syndrome.

Modern wheat varieties, especially those processed into refined flour, may be harder for some people to digest compared to ancient wheat varieties (like einkorn, emmer, or spelt). These older grains have lower gluten levels and are sometimes better tolerated by individuals with mild gluten sensitivities.

Modern wheat varieties, particularly refined wheat products like white bread, have a higher glycemic index, which means they can cause blood sugar levels to spike quickly. This has raised concerns about the contribution of modern wheat to the rising rates of type 2 diabetes and obesity.

Although wheat itself is not genetically modified, concerns have arisen about the use of glyphosate (the active ingredient in the herbicide Roundup) as a desiccant. In some parts of the United States, glyphosate is sprayed on wheat just before harvest to dry out the crop, making it easier to process.

Some consumers worry about potential health risks associated with glyphosate residue in wheat products, although regulatory bodies like the EPA maintain that the levels of glyphosate in food are safe. Still, there is ongoing debate about the long-term health effects of glyphosate exposure, with some studies linking it to potential carcinogenic effects.

As you can see, threats to our beautiful families surround us constantly, and as I keep saying, we are not focused on solutions. We are not putting the family at the center and filtering all our decision-making through it. In this upside-down model, families will continue to suffer the effects of greed and selfish agendas because we are letting it happen. In our model, the family would be at the top, and government would be underneath, serving us. Which is what governments were originally designed to do, not the other way around.

13. THE NEW SHAPE OF THE AMERICAN FAMILY

"Family is not defined by our genes, it is built and maintained through love, support, and shared commitment."
—Dr. Jerry Cammarata

It used to be that if you wanted to have a child, you had to be married, or if you wanted to have a sex life, you had to be married. These things are now available to women, regardless of marital status, and we continue to ponder and debate the issues based on the cultural values given to us at home, school, and as part of our religious teachings.

As religious views and prejudices rail against "nonconformists" to the stabilizing traditions of 'tried and true beliefs,' so is the pushback aggressively increasing. Admittedly, there are now so many legal and cultural changes that make women less dependent on marriage. Our role is to question why this independence has been brewing, and could it be the result of hundreds of years of not focusing on the family?

We are at the crossroads of really understanding the family in this country, knowing that having children should not be a deal breaker, but an honor and privilege. The role marriage has played in our country has defined who we are, yet it is understandable that there are laws and policies that offer alternatives. This discussion will be ongoing, and it is imperative that the voices on all sides become part of a solution that can intelligently be embraced by our society and grow our society.

As with all these new directions and situations, going back is just never going to fully happen and trying to force that will only create friction and conflict; history tells us that and provides us with the architecture of thoughtfulness - to make the best decisions going forward.

The shape of the family has changed and will continue to change. What we must focus on is healthy families, support for families, resources for families, whatever shape they may take, and being mindful that the number of children should be a matter of desire, not affordability, and liability.

As we have already explored, the structure of families in America has diversified significantly in recent decades. So, let's look at what these new shapes look like that are becoming more and more common.

Single-Parent Families: Families headed by one parent, either a mother or a father, raising children alone due to divorce, separation, death, or choice.

Blended Families: Families where one or both parents have children from previous relationships, and they come together to form a new family unit, often including half-siblings and stepsiblings.

Extended Families: Households that include not only parents and children but also other relatives such as grandparents, aunts, uncles, and cousins living together or in close proximity.

Cohabiting Couples: Unmarried couples living together, often raising children without the legal framework of marriage.

Same-Sex Families: Families with parents of the same gender, who may have biological, adopted, or surrogate children.

Child-Free Families: Couples who choose not to have children, focusing their lives on each other and other pursuits.

Multi-Generational Families: Families where multiple generations live under one roof, often including grandparents, parents, and children, sometimes due to economic reasons or cultural practices.

Adoptive Families: Families where one or more children have been legally adopted, creating a family unit that may include siblings from different biological backgrounds.

Foster Families: Families that provide temporary care for children who are not able to live with their biological parents, often with the potential for adoption.

Grandparent-Headed Families: Families where grandparents are the primary caregivers for their grandchildren, often due to the absence or inability of the parents to care for the children.

Co-Parenting Families: Families where two or more adults share parenting responsibilities for a child without being in a romantic relationship, often seen in cases of divorced or separated parents.

Polyamorous Families: Families that include multiple partners who share romantic relationships and may also raise children together.

Communal Families: Groups of families or individuals who live together and share resources, responsibilities, and parenting duties in a communal setting.

Military Families: Families where one or more members are active-duty military, leading to unique challenges such as frequent relocations and long periods of separation.

Transnational Families: Families where members are spread across different countries, often due to migration, with parents or children living apart but maintaining strong familial bonds across borders.

These diverse family structures reflect the changing social, economic, and cultural landscape in America, where the definition of family has broadened to include a wide variety of living arrangements and caregiving relationships.

In traditional terms, growing up without a father in the house is said to have a range of effects on children and the family as a whole, though the specific outcomes can vary widely depending on a variety of factors, including the presence of other supportive adults (the village), the financial stability of the household, and the overall family dynamic. When faced with a fatherless family, some of the factors to be aware of begin with emotional and psychological impacts that can be addressed in various ways. Let's begin with identity and self-esteem: Children may struggle with issues of identity and self-esteem, particularly boys who might lack a male role model. They may experience feelings of abandonment, leading to issues with self-worth and a sense of rejection. As always, when you are aware of potential problems you can build frameworks to avoid them.

Research has also shown that children from father-absent homes are more likely to exhibit behavioral problems, including aggression, delinquency, and a higher likelihood of engaging in risky behaviors during adolescence.

I have one friend who grew up in such a home and he went a long way down the wrong path which led to him stealing cars, dozens of arrests for various offenses, and culminated in the police taking him to a juvenile prison to show him where he was going should he continue down that path. As it turns out, he left his home city, learned a trade with his father who had returned from prison himself, and transformed himself into a very successful entrepreneur and businessman. It doesn't always go wrong, but in many ways, he was very lucky in the correctional bumps he received along the way.

Mental health is certainly another concern that must be addressed in a nontraditional family structure. There can be a higher incidence of anxiety, depression, and other mental health issues among children who grow up without a father, particularly if the father's absence is due to conflict or divorce.

Social and academic development and academic performance, as some studies suggest, can be affected if not preemptively addressed by the remaining parent. The child might have lower grades, lower educational aspirations, and a higher likelihood of dropping out of school.

Children may also have more difficulty developing social skills and forming healthy relationships with peers, particularly if they lack positive male role models. They may also be more susceptible to peer pressure.

Single-mother households are more likely to experience financial difficulties, which can limit access to resources such as quality education, extracurricular activities, and stable housing, all of which are important for healthy development.

There is obviously increased pressure on the mother who must take on both parenting roles and provide financially. This can lead to feelings of burnout and less availability for emotional support.

The absence of a father can mean a lack of a male role model, which can affect how children view gender roles and relationships. This can be mitigated if other male figures, such as uncles, grandfathers, or mentors of varying types who are involved in the child's life.

Of course there are plenty of families that are completely dysfunctional or even destructive that have fathers and mothers in place so it is not about a certain structure. It is about addressing what is missing from any structure and working out how to provide it to make it whole.

For example, children who grow up without a father may have different perspectives on relationships and family life, potentially affecting their own future relationships. They might either idealize or fear relationships based on their experiences. Being cognizant of this and all these factors is paramount because knowing what to expect and what dangers to watch for is a battle half won. Providing materials, curating entertainment, and most importantly, discussing these elements openly can have a powerful impact.

There is some evidence to suggest that children who grow up without a father are more likely to experience father absence in their own families when they become adults, perpetuating a cycle of absenteeism but it's important to note that not all children from father-absent homes experience negative outcomes. Many children demonstrate remarkable resilience and adaptability, particularly when they have strong support from their mother, extended family, and community. Or, like my friend I mentioned earlier, have a natural disposition to adapt in positive ways in adverse situations.

Other children might develop a particularly strong bond with their mother, which can provide them with emotional security and stability. Whatever happens, the impact of a father's absence can be mitigated by strong community ties, involvement in supportive social networks, and access to positive role models outside the immediate family.

In conclusion, while growing up without a father in the house can present challenges for children, the outcomes depend heavily on the broader context of the family environment, the presence of supportive adults, and the resources available to the family. Again, many children thrive despite these challenges, particularly when provided with love, support, and stability from other sources.

Now let's explore the same situation but in a motherless home. Children who grow up with a father but no mother in the home can experience a variety of emotional, social, and developmental effects, much like those seen in father-absent households, though these impacts may manifest differently.

Fathers may face unique challenges in balancing the dual roles of provider and nurturer, and while many fathers can offer strong emotional support, the absence of a mother may lead to a lack of maternal care that influences a child's emotional well-being, particularly when it comes to nurturing and empathetic behaviors typically associated with maternal figures. Children may feel a sense of loss or abandonment, which can affect their self-esteem and attachment styles in future relationships. Additionally, they may miss out on the benefits of maternal role modeling, particularly when it comes to understanding gender roles and developing balanced relationships with women. However, as with any single-parent household, the overall effects depend on the father's emotional availability, financial stability, and the presence of other supportive adults or female role models in the child's life. In supportive environments, children may still thrive and develop resilience despite the absence of a mother.

Children growing up in a home with two same-sex parents generally experience similar developmental outcomes as those raised by opposite-sex parents, provided they are raised in a loving and supportive environment. Research has shown that children of same-sex parents typically develop social skills, self-esteem, and academic abilities on par with their peers from heterosexual households. However, these children may face unique challenges, particularly related to societal stigma or discrimination, which can impact their emotional well-being. The presence of two parents, regardless of gender, provides a stable, nurturing environment where children can thrive. Importantly, same-sex parents often cultivate open communication and foster a strong sense of acceptance and diversity, which can positively influence their children's social and emotional development. In supportive communities and with access to resources, children of same-sex parents can grow up with a strong sense of identity and resilience, fully prepared to navigate the complexities of the broader world.

All structures considered, nothing does more for any family than better education, better resources, and a family-first methodology. The family dynamic is changing rapidly and will continue to do so. Our mission, should we choose to accept it, is to provide the best possible framework, infrastructure, and care to promote the foundational values of families, whatever they look like. That is, and should be, the American way.

14. HOW ARTIFICIAL INTELLIGENCE MAY AFFECT FAMILIES AND SOCIETY

"Artificial intelligence will not replace humans, but it will reshape how we live, work, and connect—forcing us to redefine what it means to be human and how we build meaningful relationships."
— Kai-Fu Lee

"The real question is not whether machines think, but whether humans can still connect meaningfully as machines take over tasks that once bonded us."
— Sherry Turkle

We explored social media and its power to help and hinder families in depth but with artificial intelligence we have a powerful new friend that could easily be a powerful new foe—the scope and scale of which is only now starting to be imagined. So, let's now consider how AI might be good for the future of American Families and how might it work against them.

We thought the internet was the most significant influence on humanity we would see in our lifetime, but AI has the potential to affect us in ways we never dreamed of. As AI itself creates better versions of AI we will soon be accelerating at a rate so fast we could easily get into unknown and dangerous territory.

To begin the exploration, let's consider how AI has the potential to significantly impact the future of American families in both positive and negative ways. Here's are some points to consider but hopefully you will add to the list as you consider our future under this new and exciting lens.

Positive Impacts on American Families

Improved Healthcare

Personalized Medicine: AI can analyze a family's medical history to provide personalized healthcare recommendations, leading to more effective treatments and preventive care.

Telemedicine and Health Monitoring: AI-powered telemedicine services can provide families with access to healthcare professionals from home, making healthcare more accessible and convenient. Wearable devices using AI can monitor health in real time, alerting families to potential health issues early.

Educational Support

Personalized Learning: AI can tailor educational content to meet each child's learning style and pace, helping students who may struggle in traditional classroom settings. This can lead to better academic outcomes and increased engagement. Class sizes and teacher bandwidth have limited the scope of individualized attention but with the help of AI, teachers could potentially create individualized curriculum to be more aligned with individual student needs.

Homework Assistance: AI-driven tutoring tools can provide on-demand support for students with their schoolwork, helping to bridge gaps in understanding and offering resources that parents might not be able to provide directly. Parents are sometimes burdened with their child's homework because they want them to succeed but quite often it is the process of working it out themselves that is most important. Like building the puzzle. AI can instantly tell them where the holes are in their knowledge and the child will feel more fulfilled executing the path for themselves.

Enhanced Family Safety

Home Security: AI-powered home security systems can provide families with advanced monitoring capabilities, such as facial recognition for identifying potential intruders and smart alerts for unusual activity.

Online Safety for Children: AI tools can help monitor children's online activities to protect them from harmful content and interactions. This can include detecting cyberbullying, inappropriate content, and potential online predators.

Work–Life Balance

Flexible Work Arrangements: AI-driven tools can facilitate remote work and flexible scheduling, allowing parents to spend more time with their children and reduce the stress of commuting.

Household Automation: AI can automate household tasks like cleaning, grocery shopping, and managing finances, giving families more time to spend together.

Financial Planning and Management

Smart Financial Tools: AI-powered budgeting apps can help families manage their finances more effectively, offering personalized advice on saving, investing, and spending based on their income and goals.

Fraud Detection: AI can monitor financial accounts for suspicious activity, protecting families from identity theft and financial fraud.

Closing Distances: Technology is anticipated to advance rapidly, revolutionizing how we connect and communicate. Families separated by distance will have new ways to stay engaged in each other's lives. Dr. Ian Pearson predicts that artificial reality will evolve to the point where people can simulate lifelike "physical" interactions without the need to travel, saving both time and money. This innovation promises to strengthen family bonds, particularly during festive occasions like Christmas, making long-distance connections feel more personal and immersive.

Negative Impacts on American Families

Privacy Concerns

Data Collection and Surveillance: AI systems often rely on collecting large amounts of personal data. This raises concerns about privacy, especially if data about family activities, health, or finances is misused or falls into the wrong hands.

Children's Privacy: With the increased use of AI in toys, educational apps, and online platforms, there is a risk of violating children's privacy by tracking their activities and behaviors.

Mental Health and Social Development

Increased Screen Time: AI-powered devices and platforms can lead to increased screen time for children, potentially impacting their mental health, social development, and physical well-being.

Social Media Algorithms: AI algorithms in social media can expose children and teens to harmful content, cyberbullying, and addictive behaviors, contributing to anxiety, depression, and social isolation.

Job Displacement

Economic Stability: AI and automation can lead to job displacement in various industries. If parents lose their jobs due to automation, it can result in financial instability and increased stress within the family.

Changing Workforce Demands: The need for new skills in an AI-driven economy may require parents to invest in further education or job training, which can be both time-consuming and costly.

Bias and Inequality

Algorithmic Bias: AI systems can perpetuate and amplify societal biases if they are trained on biased data. This can lead to discriminatory outcomes in areas like education, healthcare, and law enforcement, affecting families from marginalized communities.

Access to AI Benefits: There is a risk that the benefits of AI will be unevenly distributed, with wealthier families having more access to advanced AI tools and technologies, while lower-income families might be left behind.

Dependence on Technology

Over-Reliance: Families might become overly reliant on AI for daily tasks, potentially diminishing certain skills and human interactions. For instance, excessive reliance on AI for parenting support might reduce direct parent-child interactions.

Erosion of Human Judgment: As families start depending more on AI for decision-making in areas like healthcare, finance, and education, there's a risk of eroding human judgment and intuition, which are crucial in complex and nuanced situations.

Balancing the Impact

For AI to be beneficial to American families, careful consideration and regulation are required to ensure it is used ethically and responsibly. Policymakers, educators, and technology companies need to work together to create frameworks that protect privacy, promote digital literacy, and ensure equitable access to AI benefits. Additionally, families themselves can play a role by being mindful of how they integrate AI into their lives, using it as a tool to enhance their well-being without allowing it to dominate or negatively influence their dynamics.

If our Secretary of the Family's office were to train an AI to run all potential policy through to ascertain and weigh benefits or costs to the family we'd have a full-time filter employed to protect our interests.

Now let's explore how AI could be used directly against us. There is a danger that AI could be used to influence government leadership in various ways, raising significant concerns about the integrity of democratic processes, national security, and public trust. Here are some key areas where AI could potentially influence government leadership:

1. Manipulation of Public Opinion

Disinformation Campaigns: AI can be used to create and spread disinformation at an unprecedented scale. Through deepfakes (AI-generated fake videos and audio), bots, and AI-generated news articles, malicious actors can manipulate public opinion to sway elections, discredit political opponents, or create social unrest.

Microtargeting: AI algorithms can analyze vast amounts of data to create detailed profiles of individuals' beliefs, behaviors, and vulnerabilities. This information can be used for microtargeting political messages tailored to influence specific groups of voters, often exploiting their fears or biases to achieve desired outcomes.

2. Election Interference

Automated Propaganda: AI can be used to generate and disseminate propaganda on social media platforms. Bots can amplify divisive content, create echo chambers, and manipulate online discourse to shape political narratives. This can influence election outcomes by swaying undecided voters or demoralizing certain voter groups.

Hacking and Cyber Attacks: AI can enhance the sophistication of cyber attacks on electoral systems. These attacks can range from hacking voting machines to manipulating voter registration databases, undermining the integrity of elections and eroding public trust in democratic institutions.

3. Policy Influence and Lobbying

Automated Lobbying: AI can be used to identify and exploit weaknesses in political decision-making processes. For example, AI-driven lobbying tools can analyze legislators' voting histories, preferences, and policy priorities to tailor lobbying efforts more effectively. This can lead to disproportionate influence by certain interest groups, especially those with access to advanced AI technologies.

Policy Manipulation: AI can analyze policy proposals to identify potential loopholes or weaknesses that can be exploited by interest groups. For instance, corporations or foreign entities could use AI to craft policies that appear beneficial but have hidden provisions serving their interests.

4. Surveillance and Control

Mass Surveillance: Governments could use AI-powered surveillance systems to monitor citizens, including political opponents and activists. This can lead to suppression of dissent, erosion of privacy, and the establishment of authoritarian control.

Predictive Policing and Social Credit Systems: AI can be used to predict and preempt potential political threats or unrest. In extreme cases, governments could implement AI-driven social credit systems to reward or punish individuals based on their political behavior, effectively controlling and influencing the political landscape.

5. Influence on Political Leaders

Information Manipulation: AI can be used to feed political leaders curated information that aligns with certain agendas. For instance, AI algorithms can prioritize specific news articles, reports, or data points while suppressing others, potentially influencing leaders' perceptions and decision-making.

Deepfakes and Blackmail: Deepfake technology can be used to create convincing but false audio and video recordings of political leaders, which can be used for blackmail, coercion, or discrediting opponents. This poses a serious risk to political stability and the personal security of government officials.

6. Erosion of Trust in Leadership and Institutions

Distrust and Polarization: The use of AI to manipulate information and public opinion can lead to widespread distrust in government, media, and democratic institutions. When citizens become skeptical of all information sources, it creates fertile ground for conspiracy theories, polarization, and political instability.

Delegitimizing Political Processes: If AI is perceived as manipulating elections or policy decisions, it can delegitimize political processes. The belief that AI and algorithms, rather than the will of the people, determine political outcomes can lead to civic disengagement and a decline in democratic participation.

Mitigating the Risks

Regulation and Oversight: Governments and international organizations can establish regulations to govern the use of AI in political contexts. This includes laws against the use of deepfakes for political purposes, restrictions on data use for microtargeting, and transparency requirements for political advertising.

Promoting Digital Literacy: Educating the public about AI, digital manipulation techniques, and critical media consumption can help build resilience against disinformation and manipulation.

Ethical AI Development: Tech companies and AI developers can adopt ethical guidelines to prevent the misuse of AI for manipulating political processes. This includes building safeguards into AI systems and promoting transparency in AI applications.

Strengthening Cybersecurity: Protecting electoral systems, government databases, and critical infrastructure from AI-enhanced cyber attacks is crucial for safeguarding democratic processes.

International Collaboration: Since AI-driven influence campaigns can cross borders, international cooperation is necessary to address the global nature of these threats, including coordinated efforts to counter disinformation and cyber threats.

While AI holds the potential for improving government efficiency and data-aided decision-making, its misuse poses significant risks to democratic governance and the integrity of political processes. Addressing these challenges requires a combination of technological safeguards, policy interventions, and public awareness.

Until now, we did not have a reference source readily available at our fingertips. Political leaders, for example, could create policies with agendas unknown and without heavy research and resources, we had no way to easily or efficiently cross check political strategies or to qualify what we were being told is true or in our best interests. Imagine now, if we began using AI to cross-check political decision-making. Another voice in the room, potentially impartial—to a point—data and research driven, and all at the push of a button. Here are some possible applications for its use in the field of political accountability.

Fact-Checking and Analysis

AI can analyze political statements and policies to identify inaccuracies or inconsistencies. By comparing claims to massive databases of facts, statistics, and historical data, AI can quickly verify the veracity of policy claims made by politicians.

Policy Impact Simulation

AI models can simulate the potential impact of proposed policies by analyzing historical data, economic models, and social trends. For example, AI can project the economic effects of a new tax policy or the environmental impact of proposed regulations.

Bias Detection

AI can analyze policy proposals and political rhetoric for signs of bias or manipulation. This can include identifying loaded language, propaganda techniques, or the potential impact on different demographic groups.

Cross-Referencing with Existing Laws and Policies

AI can cross-check new policy proposals against existing laws and regulations to identify conflicts, redundancies, or gaps. This can help ensure that new policies are consistent with the current legal framework. Yes, we have lawyers for this but we are talking about real time monitoring here, key performance indicators to help nudge our course and provide instant accountability.

Public Opinion Analysis

By analyzing social media, news articles, and public forums, AI can gauge public sentiment and reaction to political policies. This can provide a real-time check on how different segments of the population view proposed policies.

Ethical Considerations and Fairness

AI can be programmed to assess policies from an ethical standpoint by considering human rights, fairness, and social justice implications. For example, it can evaluate the fairness of healthcare or immigration policies.

Comparative Policy Analysis

AI can compare policies across different countries or regions to highlight best practices or cautionary tales. This can help policymakers understand how similar policies have fared in other contexts.

Data-Driven Decision-Making

AI can help ensure that policy decisions are data-driven by analyzing large datasets to provide insights into complex issues such as climate change, healthcare, and education.

While AI can significantly aid in cross-checking political policies, it's important to note that AI systems themselves can have biases based on the data they are trained on, and the algorithms used. Therefore, human oversight and transparency in AI processes are crucial.

In his recent book, The Singularity is Nearer—an update of his 2005 book the Singularity is Near—Ray Kurtzweil predicts several significant milestones in our journey with AI. He predicts that:

1. By 2029, machines will pass a Turing test demonstrating they have human-level cognitive ability and will become indistinguishable from a human conversation.
2. By 2030, we will have brain-computer interfaces and human augmentation.
3. During early 2030s, Kurzweil anticipates breakthroughs in biotechnology and nanotechnology that will lead to significant advancements in human health, the reversal of aging, and the extension of human life spans. He has suggested that some people alive today could live indefinitely as these technologies mature.
4. By 2045, The Singularity: Kurzweil's most famous prediction is that by 2045, the technological singularity will occur. This is the moment when artificial intelligence will surpass human intelligence, leading to unprecedented technological growth and the merging of human and machine intelligence.

Kurzweil also states that when we first gained access to the prefrontal cortex, this is when we became human. With a human-machine interface we effectively connect to a giant prefrontal cortex in the cloud giving us instant access to all available information at the speed of thought. An indisputable evolution of human ability that makes us something else. This interaction will in turn change the brains own inherent cognitive ability potentially making us something beyond human.

If Kurzweil is correct on any one of his futurist assumptions, we have a lot to prepare for to ready ourselves and our families for such things. It creates more questions than answers about how we might deal with life extension mentally, economically, morally, and spiritually. If the first person to live beyond 122 or to 1000 is alive today, then we don't have much time to get ourselves in shape to deal with such questions and acceleration.

What will families look like with dramatic life extension, cognitive abilities rivaling quantum computing, and the ability to access all knowledge by thinking about it? It is exciting to look to the future and imagine but it is also a lot to take in. To comprehend such an existential shift during our lifetimes is not something we have ever been called to do. On the other hand, it is a pleasant relief from worrying about current day-to-day dilemmas like the threat of civil war, who will and should be the next president, and the ever illusive quest for a peaceful world.

Maybe we would be better off if the machines ran things. We do seem to create more and more problems for ourselves. But let's get back to our current quest in this adventure, the quest for the future of the American family.

15. THE WHITEHOUSE CONFERENCE ON FAMILIES

LISTENING TO AMERICA'S FAMILIES

"The strength of a nation lies in the homes of its people. To lead effectively, leaders must first listen to the voices of families—the heart of every community."
— Franklin D. Roosevelt

Here are some excerpts from the overview booklet of the original Whitehouse Conference on Families. The original document can be seen by scanning the QR code.

Excerpt: This illustrated booklet for delegates provides a very brief overview of the White House Conference on Families. Contents include a welcoming statement by the conference chairperson, a review of preconference activities leading up to the conference, and lists of conference goals and themes.

Welcome letter by President Carter

THE WHITE HOUSE WASHINGTON
May 27, 1980

I wish to congratulate you on your selection as delegates to the White House Conference on Families. Your participation will enrich and strengthen this unique process of listening to American families. This conference is a long overdue examination of how our major institutions help, hurt, or ignore families. You carry with you the hopes and concerns of thousands of Americans who believe families have been overlooked for too long. Working together, I am confident we can build upon the strengths of our families, recognize their diverse needs, and take real action to develop more responsive and sensitive policies toward them. I look forward with great anticipation to the results of this Conference, and I thank you for your special help in this critical and challenging task.

[signature: Jimmy Carter]

A message from Jim Guy Tucker
Chairperson, White House Conference on Families

No previous White House Conference has been convened to deal with problems that are as compelling and as profound as those facing this White House Conference on Families.

Families have always been this nation's fundamental institution and source of strength. They are certainly our most precious asset because within "ordinary" American families, an extraordinary thing takes place: our nation's future is shaped and formed. Our families have done that job exceedingly well, often under trying circumstances.

But at no time in our history have families been under more pressure than they are today. Pounded by successive waves of deep and often uncreditable change, they have had to meet their day-to-day needs while struggling with government, with other institutions, and frequently with each other as well. Too often, government, whether in the Nation's Capital or in a small town's city hall, has compounded the problem by creating public policies and programs-in taxation, education, social welfare, and so on—that work to a family's disadvantage.

Some have said that this Conference will be an invitation for further Government control of family life. I believe just the opposite. Government steps in when families cannot help themselves; the overriding goal of the White House Conference on Families is to ensure that every family is strong enough to stand alone. To me, stronger families mean less government, not more.

But we cannot turn our backs on families in need. It remains the responsibility of government to help when all other means have failed.

In calling the White House Conference on Families, President Carter directed that every effort be made to reach out to all Americans so that we could listen to them—and learn from them. This, I believe, we have done successfully. But I want to remind you that our gathering together here does not mark the end of an effort but the beginning of an even larger and more challenging undertaking—the responsibility of translating this Conference's recommendations into reality.

Along with my fellow members of the National Advisory Committee and the WHCF staff, I look forward to sharing that responsibility with you.

America's Families Speak out

Concerned by what he perceived as the lack of national policy to strengthen families, President Carter convened the White House Conference on Families to "examine the strengths of American families, the difficulties they face, and the ways in which family life is affected by public policies." He directed that the Conference "reach out, not only to scholars and to experts. but to many thousands of Americans around the country who know from their own experience what makes a family strong." Because of this, the White House Conference on Families is different from any White House Conference of the past.

It was preceded by seven national hearings, a National Research Forum on Family Issues, and by more than 300 state events in which more than 100,000 people participated. It will be followed by a period of intensive advocacy that has been called for by both the President and by the Congress.

During the summer of 1979, the National Advisory Committee established goals and themes for the Conference and devised a process of participation that distinguishes this White House Conference from all others. Instead of focusing activities on a single event. as previous Conferences had done, the Committee designed a program of national, state, and local activities intended to give all Americans an opportunity to speak out on what they think is right and wrong with the public and private policies that affect their lives.

To start the listening process, the Conference held national hearings across the country between September 1979 and January 1980; there were seven in all: Kansas City and Lindsborg, Kansas; Nashville and Memphis, Tennessee; Denver, Colorado; Hartford and Stamford, Connecticut; Washington, D.C.; Detroit, Michigan; and Seattle, Washington. While the hearings' planners anticipated modest attendance, more than 4,000 persons—single-working parents, college students, senior citizens living in poverty, teenage mothers, family care professionals, and elected officials—turned out, often at a personal sacrifice.

The thrust of their testimony was enormously positive. Americans from every walk of life, of all races, of every political and philosophical persuasion, testified their deep and abiding faith in the family as the primary source of strength in an increasingly complex society. But they voiced many deep concerns as well.

That most frequently cited was the sensitivity—or lack of it—of federal, state, and local government toward families. Many criticized tax, welfare, health, and foster care policies that ignore or undermine families. Others accused government of ignoring racial or ethnic differences and the structural diversity of families, and noted the lack of accessibility to, and accountability for, government services.

The second most frequently stated concern was economic. Inflation and poverty—and just trying to make it on an average income—are creating terrible pressures on American families, stresses that too frequently result in divorce, alcoholism, or violence.

The third major concern was support for specific family structures that exist today-and the need for major institutions, including government to recognize this diversity in designing policies and programs.

Other concerns most frequently voiced at the national hearings included: the scarcity of affordable childcare, particularly for working parents; the quality of health care; conflicts between work and family responsibilities; the need for family life education; the relationships between parents and their children; and the roles of community institutions in supporting families.

The Conference listening process next focused on state activities, which began in the fall of 1979 and concluded in April 1980. Virtually every state, the District of Columbia, Puerto Rico, and American territories convened hearings, forums, and conferences to identify leading family concerns and recommend changes in public and private policies. The resulting state reports were instrumental in preparing the Conference agenda.

The states were given another, crucially important responsibility: selection of more than 80% of the 2,000 delegates to the Conferences through a unique combination of peer selection and gubernatorial appointment. The vast majority of the delegates are not professionals serving families, but family members themselves, and, as the following figures show, closely reflect the nation's population:

- 25% represent racial minorities;
- Nearly 13% are single parents;
- 8% are over 60 years old;
- 10% are from low-income families; and
- More than 4% are handicapped.

The States' outstanding performance in reaching out to people and in selecting delegates is quite remarkable considering that no Federal funds were available to assist these efforts.

Two other pre-Conference events are noteworthy. On April 10–11, 1980, the Conference held a National Research Forum on Family Issues in Washington, D.C. Leading scholars and experts from the private and public sectors highlighted what is known about families and, more importantly, identified areas where further research is needed.

To complete the development of a broad base of facts and viewpoints to aid the delegates, a Gallup Poll on American Families was undertaken. The results of this first national comprehensive poll on American families will be shared with the delegates at all three Conference sites.

National organizations and the business community have also been significantly involved in the White House Conference on Families.

More than 250 national organizations, ranging from the American Red Cross and the Future Homemakers of America to the National Council on Churches and the National Council on Aging, urged their members to participate in Conference hearings and state activities. Many also submitted formal statements of their major family concerns for consideration by delegates to the National Conferences.

Conference Deputy Chair Donald Seibert, who is also Chairman and Chief Executive Officer of the J.C. Penney Co., Inc., fanned a Business Task Force in 1979 to encourage business support for the Conference. With representatives of more than two dozen major corporations, the Task Force contributed substantive issues input to the Conference and also raised funds for special Conference projects.

During the Conferences, delegates from 57 States and territories will review and discuss major issues and vote on Conference recommendations. The issues have been grouped into four major areas:

Families and Economic Well-Being

- Economic Pressures
- Families and Work
- Tax Policies
- Income Security for Families
- Status of Homemakers

Family Challenges and Responsibilities

- Preparation for Marriage and Family Life
- Specific Supports for Families
- Parents and Children
- Family Violence
- Substance Abuse
- Aging and Families

Families and Human Needs

- Education
- Health
- Housing
- Childcare
- The Handicapped

Families and Major Institutions

- Government
- Television
- Community Institutions
- Law and the Judicial System.

At the conclusion of the three national Conferences, a 117-member National Task Force will meet to consolidate these recommendations into a single final report, which is to be completed by the end of August 1980.

Following this there will be a six-month effort to turn the Conference's recommendations into action. Activities will include a report to the President, meetings with key Federal agency officials and Congressional leaders, and wide distribution of the Conference recommendations. The conference participants will also receive reports of all the results of the White House Conference.

Conference Goals

The National Advisory Committee to the White House Conference on Families has adopted the following goals for the Conference:

1. To initiate broad nationwide discussions of families in the United States.
2. To develop a process of listening to and involving families themselves, especially those families that have too often been left out of the formulation of policies that affect their lives.
3. To share what is known about families—their importance, diversity, strengths, problems. responses to a changing world, etc.—and to generate and share new knowledge about families.
4. To identify public policies, institutional actions and other factors that may harm or neglect family life, to determine differing impact on particular groups, and to recommend new policies designed to strengthen and support families.
5. To stimulate and encourage a wide variety of activities in neighborhoods, grass-roots organizations, communities, states, national organizations, media, and other public and private groups focused on supporting and strengthening families and individuals within families.
6. To examine the impact of economic forces (poverty, unemployment. inflation. etc.) on families, with special emphasis and involvement of poor families.
7. To encourage diverse groups of families to work together through local, state, and national networks and other institutions for policies which strengthen and support family life.
8. To generate interest in and action on Conference recommendations among individuals, families, and governmental and non-governmental bodies at every level. (These activities will include monitoring and evaluation efforts.)

Conference Themes

The National Advisory Committee on the White House Conference on Families has adopted the following themes as starting points or principles for discussion of issues:

Family Strengths and Supports

Families are the oldest, most fundamental human institution, our most precious national resource. Families serve as a source of strength and support for their members and for our society.

Diversity of Families

American families are pluralistic in nature. Our discussion of issues will reflect an understanding of and respect for cultural, ethnic, and regional differences as well as differences in structure and lifestyle.

The Changing Realities of Family Life

American society is dynamic, constantly changing. The roles of families and individual family members are growing, adapting, and evolving in new and different ways to meet the challenges of our age.

The Impact of Public and Private Institutional Policies on Families

The policies of government and major private institutions have profound effects on families. Increased sensitivity to the needs of families is needed, as well as ongoing research and action to address the negative impacts of public and private institutional policies.

The Impact of Discrimination

Many families are exposed to various and diverse forms of discrimination. These can affect individual family members as well as the family unit as a whole.

Families with Special Needs

Certain families have special needs, and these needs often produce unique strengths. The needs of families with handicapped members, single-parent families, elderly families, and many other families with special needs will be addressed during the Conference.

16. THE WHITE HOUSE CONFERENCE ON FAMILIES—RECOMMENDATIONS AND CONCLUSIONS

BY BONNIE SHANE—UNIVERSITY OF BALTIMORE LAW FORUM

"Good governance begins with hearing the voices of those it serves. A government that listens to its families lays the foundation for a stronger, more equitable future."
— Barack Obama

This is an excerpt from the Baltimore Law Forum. For the full original paper, scan the QR code to the left.

"The country is looking to you for constructive suggestions about how our society can help, not just government, but our entire society."

President Jimmy Carter used these words to launch the first White House Conference on Families (WHCF) in Baltimore on June 5, 1980. How the "constructive suggestions" will be realized, with a look at the formation of the White House Conferences on the Family and its recommendations, is timely for those concerned with the directions of the family in the 1980s. The National Advisory Committee (NAC), a diverse group of presidential appointees including professors, attorneys, religious leaders, corporation leaders, labor leaders and directors of various community agencies and organizations, met in July 1979 to organize the Conference. The first step was to establish seven national hearings across the country to focus on the concerns of the Conferences. These open hearings were buttressed by a parallel Gallop Poll entitled "American Families-1980." Then, more than 2,000 Americans, chosen by their states and their peers, participated in the three conferences held in Baltimore, Minneapolis, and Los Angeles. The delegates to those conferences agreed on over 170 recommendations which were compiled and reported by a National Task Force. The Task Force is currently in an implementation process which will run until March 1981, in an effort to realize the recommendations. The top recommendations ranked in order of overall concern were: Family Oriented Personnel Policy Implementation Substance Abuse Prevention Tax Revision to Support Families Tax Policies for Care of Aging and Handicapped Family Impact Analysis Public Awareness of Handicapping Conditions Government Programs to Assist Handicapped Home Care for Elderly Tax Credits for Aging

Recommendations

Families and Major Institutions

Government

The conferences all showed deep concern about government sensitivity for families. The number one recommendation in Minneapolis was "that laws and regulations be analyzed in terms of their impact on families." All supported ratification of the Equal Rights Amendment. Media All three conferences expressed concern about media influence on the family. They called for greater regulation by the Federal Communications Commission (FCC), with more community consultation, and less emphasis on violence, pornography, crime, stereotyping, drugs, and alcohol. Specific recommendations requested the FCC to establish regional grievance mechanisms, community advisory boards and to promote an understanding and awareness of disabled persons. Community Institutions Each conference sought greater involvement of community and religious organizations in planning and providing services to assist families, and encouragement of self-help groups. Attacks on racism and discrimination were recommended. Law and Judicial System Baltimore and Los Angeles delegates urged greater use of conciliation services in family disputes and a system of special family courts, as well as arbitration and mediation, as alternatives to traditional adversary courtroom settlement of marital disputes. The Minneapolis group made no recommendations concerning family law and the judicial system, but instead, formed proposals to support a Human Life Amendment and to oppose the Equal Rights Amendment. (Both were defeated by the Conference.)

Families and Human Needs

Education

In Los Angeles, the number one recommendation called for a school-parent partnership to ensure quality education. All Conferences showed interest in developing educational policies and suggested establishing community advisory councils, Family Education Programs, Community Education Programs, and equal education opportunities with state and federal government assistance.

Health

Here again, Minneapolis did not pass a recommendation. (Three recommendations opposing abortion were defeated.) Baltimore and Los Angeles expressed concern about improving health care through education, early intervention, counseling, and screening.

Childcare

There was consistent agreement on the need for alternative forms of quality childcare and full parental choices. Several recommendations dealt with enactment of incentives for businesses who sponsor childcare.

The Handicapped

Many recommendations from all three conferences concerned families with members who suffer from handicaps. The use of the media, education, training, counseling, and self-help groups was suggested to promote positive attitudes. Delegates also proposed the use of tax credits to encourage home care of disabled family members.

Housing

Affordable housing, programs to end housing discrimination, and strict enforcement of current laws to eliminate discrimination were proposals adopted by each WHCF.

Family Challenges and Responsibilities

Drug Substance Abuse

The top Baltimore recommendation concerned drug substance abuse and steps that schools, the media, parents and health professionals could take to alleviate and control this serious problem. The other two conferences showed deep concern and expressed the need for training qualified personnel, government assistance, and accessibility of treatment. A specific

Minneapolis recommendation proposed an increase in alcohol taxes to fund local treatment programs.

Aging

With belief that the individuality of elderly persons should be recognized through a broad choice of living arrangements, all conferences suggested provision for home as well as institutional settings. Tax incentives to households with elderly members were strongly recommended. Suggested reforms in the social security system included assurance of an adequate income level, reduction of limitation on earned income and no reduction in social security payments because of marriage.

Parents and Children

Recommendations concerning adolescent pregnancies ranged from comprehensive health, education and social services to positive peer group values as a means of prevention. All agreed that in the area of foster care and adoption each child has a right to a stable, permanent home.

Preparation for Marriage and Family Life

There was unanimous support for "comprehensive family life education for children, youth and adults," with courses and programs in human development, marriage and the family, parenting, and human sexuality suggested. Family Violence The need for government leadership in understanding the cause of family violence and in enacting and funding protective legislation was emphasized. A need to increase public awareness through media and community education was stressed. Rehabilitation services for the victim and the perpetrator of family violence were recommended.

Families and Economic Well-Being

Status of Homemakers

Recommendations supported changes in the tax code, including elimination of state and federal inheritance taxes for spouses, as well as tax credits for homemakers providing primary care for handicapped and elderly persons, and were approved by overwhelming majorities at all three conferences.

Increased recognition of and equity for full-time homemakers through tax and social security changes were called for.

Income Security

Specific proposals for changes in the social security system included survivor benefits regardless of age and children, credit for time taken off from work for child rearing, widow benefits at age 55, and social security benefits in one's own name rather than as dependent. While the conferences noted that income maintenance programs have a detrimental effect on families, they agreed that laws should encourage a father in indigent circumstances to remain in the household. Other proposals included "guaranteed annual income", elimination of mandatory retirement and an increase in employment opportunities for the elderly.

Economic Pressures

There was strong consensus on proposals for full employment (implementation of the Humphrey-Hawkins Act), special emphasis on lower cost of health care, food, and housing, vigorous enforcement of existing laws concerning affirmative action programs, equal pay for equal work and efforts to combat sexual harassment and discrimination.

Families and Work

Creative work arrangements such as flextime, jobsharing, flexible leave policies for both sexes and dependent care options including childcare centers received the highest recommendation from all the conferences.

Tax Policies

Nearly all the delegates called for elimination of the marriage tax penalty by permitting married couples with both spouses gainfully employed the option of filing separate or joint tax returns and tax incentives for home care for the elderly and disabled.

Implementation

WHCF staff plans for implementation include meetings with officials of the executive and legislative branches of state and federal government at all

levels, corporation leaders and community groups. Although the implementation period has begun recently, some positive responses have occurred.
President Carter proposed a reduction of marriage tax. The Senate Finance
Committee called for elimination of the marriage tax by allowing use of
either joint or individual tax returns, in H.R. 3601, proposed by Millicent
Fenwick, with 230 co-signers. Formation of a drug abuse program for government employees and their families is expected. A corporate task force
composed of 100 representatives of the largest employers is involved in
planning to make the workplace more responsive and meeting with representatives from the Departments of Labor and Commerce to consider personnel policies involving flextime, shared jobs, leave policies, etc. A report
to the Association of Family Conciliation Court is being prepared, outlining
the proposed implementation of recommendations concerning the family
within the court system. The creation of a privately funded organization
to carry out implementation and advocacy efforts on behalf of families on
an ongoing basis is in the formative stages. A number of governors have
set up state-wide speaker services that are available to children, youth, and
families on pertinent topics. The WHCF staff is using its short implementation period to encourage immediate results and working to assure that key
groups with specific interests, such as the Maryland Coalition of Families,
are aware of recommendations that coincide with their concerns in the
hope that they will continue to lobby for implementation even after the
March 1981 close of WHCF. There is a growing coalition of people working
to improve the condition of the aged and the issues raised by the WHCF
should form a basis for the White House Conference on the Aged to be held
in 1981. A family impact analysis regarding any legislation affecting families has been requested in response to the complaint that the government
interferes too much in family life. A potential problem involves the media
recommendations. There is a strong possibility of conflict with the First
Amendment rights of free speech and press. However, the conferences are
deeply concerned with programming that tends to "glorify" drugs, alcohol,
and violence, and hope that a strong group working with the media could
resolve some of these issues.

Conclusion

Centering on the simple concept of the family, WHCF is another voice
added to the call for solutions to major domestic issues in the United States.

Immediate results cannot be expected to follow from these conferences alone. It is not known whether any of the recommendations will become reality. But the conferences have brought out the many interests and concerns of American families and generated a great deal of interest, public and private. 'HARVEY CAREY DZODIN, The White House Conference on Families; The End of the Beginning, A Report to the Assoc. of Family Conciliation Courts; The White House Conference on Families, (in press).

* * *

As you can see, for all intents and purposes, the White House Conference on Families was a well-executed and well-intentioned initiative. From the conclusions, you'd have to assume it was an unmitigated success but 40 years later, why do I consider the outcomes a major disappointment? For one, the politics and follow through of the White House policies became then "same old, same old." Plenty of good came out of it as when there is strong focus there are always outcomes, but with political agendas come corruption in the focus, the process, or the execution and in the end, the WHCF agenda was not to improve the essential needs of the family, rather, to move the country values back to the middle/right.

Like many government initiatives, administrations change, momentum is lost, or we just mess up the end game. This is why I strongly advocate—through the narrative, intention, and follow thought of this book—to begin an initiative to reestablish the WHCF with renewed vim and vigor and make it the sole directive of a newly appointed portfolio director, The Secretary of Family Wellbeing, for example, so that momentum continues, and it becomes an unstoppable force for the family going forward. Whatever families may look like, whatever shape they take, they will still be a foundational part of our society so whatever we can do to make them succeed in every sense of the word, is a great thing for America. Who doesn't want to be a part of a society that honestly and unequivocally has you and your family's well-being at the foundational seat of everything we strive for?

Although, at the time of this writing, President Carter is 100, it was 40+ years ago (1980) that President Carter appointed Coretta Scott King, me, and others to his very special White House Conference on Families. He saw then, what is still difficult to recognize even today, that to understand the American Family, keeping the American Family as the centerpiece of our democracy, you must have an unbridled policy to help the family grow and give greatness in every way to our country. My first paternity leave in the nation became part of the conversation during President Carter's WHCF.

Although the 40+-year battle to get a National Paid Family Leave Policy is still part of our political landscape of indecision, President Carter ignited the flame that will soon brighten the lives of all parents and their families— hoping in the next presidential administration.

I'm proud to be a small part of American History!

17. WHAT TO DO ABOUT IT
PLANS TO CREATE A VIBRANT AMERICAN FAMILY

"The future of America depends on strong families, and strong families are built through love, opportunity, and the unwavering commitment to help every child and parent thrive."
— Marian Wright Edelman

When I was with the Giuliani administration as Commissioner of the Department of Youth and Community Development, I had a chart of all the city agencies, and in the chart, what I found was that hundreds and hundreds of millions of dollars were being earmarked for family and children-oriented activities, but they were all being duplicated.

The fire department wanted to do something, the police department wanted to do something, my agency wanted to do something. But there was nobody to coordinate how all that money was being spent in a very meaningful way so that you could really make a difference.

And I think if we looked at that across the United States and looked at all of the agencies within the federal government, you'd see the same thing; A lot of people spending a lot of money, but who is in place there coordinating to see that the family is getting the best bang for their buck?

This is why revisiting the idea of creating a new portfolio and having the position called something like The Secretary of Family Wellbeing, or The Secretary of the American Family would be a brilliant idea politically, from a campaign perspective. The secretary would have no responsibility whatsoever in the running of the entire country but every policy, every act, every law that comes out of the chambers of every secretary would have to go through the Family-Filter to review its applicability as to how would it affect the most important unit in our society. State governors would appoint such a person in local governments like New York City as the needs will certainly vary depending on the urban environment. Alas, there is nothing is happening to do such a thing, and I see it is a gaping hole in strategy. The

115

government is in place to serve the people and maintain our way of life so what have you done for the family lately?

It's probably not happening because it's easier to talk about tax credits and some of these smaller and more readily achievable things. Once you break it all down and get down to the big issues, there is only one big issue at the heart of all this. The huge, thousand-pound elephant in the room. The American Family. Reinstating The White House Conference on Families would be a huge step in the right direction, helping to map the course for the portfolio.

It would be unprecedented, but it is highly tangible and realistic. Law by law, bill by bill, align everything to the best interest of the American family to make some meaningful changes in the way things get done.

* * *

In my work as a member of the central board of education and Commissioner of DYCD I advocated to have a community office in every school. Why? Public schools are so accessible and omnipresent in NYC. Yes, we have 311 to get information on the phone, but if there was a community office in every school, parents or anyone in the community could be more connected in person with getting their quality of life imported. This office could now be redefined in our family model of accessibility and called the Community Family Access Center (CFAC).

This could be duplicated around the country. The person at the desk would have full access to every agency, department, etc., to get a solution to a problem. This would be the same as the solution of 311; however, the live component personalizes the government of the area. Or could this be achieved with AI enabling a centralized source that behaves with local context making it seem localized but with the efficiency of centralization? These are the ideas that can be developed by the WHCF and the office of the Secretary of the Family.

Imagine if you could walk into the Federal Department of Education in Washington D.C., and find a desk where you could get an answer to your quality-of-life education issue. Why not?

Washington's departments should have a groundfloor desk of essential assistance. EA (essential assistance) also means "each" person deserves helps!

But change in government won't come from electing a president. A change in the way government operates from a values perspective will require an immense, bottom-up change in how we as Americans behave, what we want from leaders, and those types of leaders emerging. I am encouraged by what I see in the leaders of tomorrow, our youth. There is a new documentary called Girl State that reveals a generation of young people who are obsessed with positive change and creating a leadership dynamic for the future. New generations are just not having this "we've always done it this way" lethargy. They do care for the environment, they do have a moral compass, and they are not interested or putting up with greed or selfish agendas.

Younger generations, especially Millennials and Generation Z, have been developing a more critical and nuanced view of government and leadership compared to older generations. Key factors shaping their views include distrust in traditional institutions. Many young people, particularly Gen Z, express a lack of faith in government institutions, seeing them as slow-moving, corrupt, or out of touch. Events like financial crises, political scandals, and mishandling of public health crises (e.g., the COVID-19 pandemic) have fueled this sentiment.

They demand more transparency from leaders and expect accountability when things go wrong.

Both Millennials and Gen Z are highly focused on issues like climate change, racial justice, gender equality, and mental health. They expect governments and leaders to prioritize these issues and are often frustrated when they see inaction.

Young people are taking matters into their own hands, leading movements like Fridays for Future (climate activism), Black Lives Matter, and various digital rights campaigns, seeking to influence change outside of traditional political frameworks.

Younger generations are more inclined to follow decentralized leadership models found in social media influencers, grassroots activists, and content creators rather than looking to traditional political figures for guidance. They favor collaborative, non-hierarchical leadership styles, where leaders are seen as facilitators or supporters rather than top-down authority figures. They also tend to be less loyal to traditional political parties. They are more likely to support policies and leaders based on issue alignment rather than party affiliation. This shift is driven by frustration with partisan gridlock, especially in the United States. A significant portion of young voters identify as independents or are skeptical of both major parties. More and more, they see themselves as global citizens and are more interested in how global governance structures, like the UN or climate accords, address issues that affect them, rather than just national governments.

Their concerns, like climate change, are global, pushing them to value leaders who engage in international cooperation, and they expect government leadership to reflect the diversity of the population, in terms of race, gender, and background. They are quick to critique institutions and leaders that fail to embody inclusivity.

The new generations prefer leaders who understand and address the interconnectedness of different social issues, such as how race, gender, and economic status overlap and they want leaders who understand technology and its potential to address modern challenges. They are also concerned about digital privacy and data misuse, holding leaders accountable for tech-related policies. They expect governments to rely more on science and data to make informed policy decisions, especially concerning healthcare, environmental policy, and education.

These emerging attitudes reflect a complex relationship between younger generations and the government, marked by both frustration and hope for new forms of leadership that better align with their values and concerns.

But how is this happening? Why are new generations seemingly wiser and more social and community-focused? Well, probably because we did such an appalling job before them that they were compelled to rail against us. Each generation seems to rail and rebel against the former. We did it to our conservative parents and drove the 60s and the hippy movement. Now, new generations are looking at the world and saying, "This is a disaster! We have to do something." And rightly so. It is a disaster. But at least we can begin the work of instilling a new framework for family values and we can do it with their help. If not now, when? If not us, who?

As always, education is the only way forward. I believe that one of the most important items on the agenda for out conference on families will be the reconfiguration of education. There is already talk of dismantling the DOE. While this measure seems drastic, with all change, opportunities present themselves. I would advocate for a shift in the US education system toward localized control and reduced federal bureaucracy. The main points might include:

Local Education Focus: Education should address local needs and involve parents, even educating them when necessary. This localized approach ensures education is relevant and impactful.

Role of the Federal Department of Education: The federal department should primarily oversee and maintain basic educational standards nationwide. Accreditation and strict standards for educational disciplines should be handled by accrediting associations, as authorized by the department of education; however, communities and states take responsibility for education beyond the basics.

Academic Required Partnerships: Education should be a partnership among states, local businesses, families, and universities. Pairing schools with local universities is presented as a revolutionary, accountable model that enhances education quality and responsibility. I think there must be a contractual relationship between colleges, high, elementary, and nursery schools in the continuum of education. The colleges teach the teacher to teach, they should, therefore work to make education better at all levels.

Future Vision: The proposed model aligns with a broader initiative to prioritize the American family, positioning their book as a "must-read" for advancing these ideas.

In summary, the emphasis is on decentralization, local partnerships, and innovative educational models to better serve communities and families.

18. THE FAMILY ACTION MANIFESTO

The foundational list for action that will underpin our White House Conference On Families. Together, we will add to and refine it into an executable plan that cannot be stopped, cannot be silenced. Below, you will be able to scan a code to download a letter template that can be sent to Congress advocating for the family and the changes that must come to provide for its future. You will also find a code to scan that will enable your own stories about family to be added to our list. Here is our top 60 beginning with our top 5 immutable must-have items.

1. **Create a Secretary of the Family - Cabinet Position**
2. **Commence a White House Conference on Families**
3. **A National Paid Family Leave Policy (No talk, action—finally)**
4. **Establish the National Education Contract (NEC)—local Colleges, high schools, elementary schools, Pre-K schools, and special education schools, must all participate in the Pre-K to 16 education of every student, all as a part of the reconfiguration of the Federal Department of Education. A local education success initiative.**
5. **Incentivize corporate America to redesign and restructure the workplace to honor the family worker.**

6. Propose increased tax benefits and credits for families with children. #financial
7. Promote access to affordable housing options for families. #financial
8. Support policies that encourage savings and financial literacy for future family stability. #financial
9. Advocate for accessible, high-quality early childhood education. #education
10. Support funding for after-school programs and extracurricular activities that are coordinated with the school's curricula. #education
11. Encourage reforms in student loan policies to reduce the financial burden on families. #education

12. Promote mental health awareness and accessible family counseling services. #Mental Health and Wellness
13. Support policies for affordable healthcare and mental health services for families. #Mental Health and Wellness
14. Encourage wellness programs that support family dynamics and reduce stress. #Mental Health and Wellness
15. Develop resources for managing screen time and promoting healthy technology use. #Technology Guidelines
16. Advocate for policies that protect children from online risks and data exploitation. #Technology Guidelines
17. Encourage digital literacy programs that educate families on safe internet use. #Technology Guidelines
18. Promote community programs that support family bonding and social connections. #Community, #education
19. Encourage the development of family centers and local resource hubs. #Community, #education
20. Support initiatives that create multi-generational support systems within communities. #Community, #education
21. Advocate for family life education as part of the school curriculum. #Family-Centric Education, #education
22. Support programs that teach parenting skills and family relationship management. #Family-Centric Education, #education
23. Encourage shared parenting responsibilities through public awareness campaigns. #Equal Parenting
24. Advocate for paternity leave policies and promote awareness of fathers' roles. #Equal Parenting
25. Promote voter awareness on family-related issues. #Civic Engagement, #education
26. Support initiatives that engage families in local and national advocacy. #Civic Engagement
27. Encourage family participation in community service and civic activities. #Civic Engagement
28. Encourage family involvement in sustainable living practices. #Sustainability
29. Support policies for accessible green spaces and family-friendly environmental programs. #Sustainability
30. Advocate for environmental education that engages families in conservation efforts. #Sustainability

31. Envision the businesses of tomorrow becoming their own schools. Liberal arts education will be handled in high school as the curriculum there gets redesigned, but education on the job is just going to be better for a significant percentage of people. Start your life earlier and without debt. Colleges and universities will contract with companies or state education departments who will accredit them. This will certainly disrupt higher education but will invoke dramatic improvements in the administration, costs, and style of college operations. #Education

32. Study the effects of governmental red tape stifling the growth and prosperity of the American family. #Efficiency

33. Discuss the truth about the amount of energy we need as a country and the process to get that energy at the lowest cost to the American family while at the same time showing how our logical investment into alternate fuels will grow, how our universities and private partners will grow this industry, how fossil fuel companies will start a retraining program for its workers to transition to alternate fuel jobs, and how this is all done with the mindfulness of the need for the American family to succeed. #Energy

34. Build a model of what society would look like if families averaged three to five kids and parents had a three-day work week.

35. Study sustainable high risers with all-inclusive services, from houses of worship, schools, stores, work, etc., the family center of the future.

36. Advocate for comprehensive family health programs that address chronic diseases and preventive care tailored to diverse family needs. #HealthAndWellness

37. Expand support for families with members who have disabilities, including accessible housing, education, and employment opportunities. #HealthAndWellness

38. Propose universal basic income trials targeted at families to evaluate the potential impact on stability and well-being. #EconomicEmpowerment

39. Encourage corporate social responsibility initiatives that support employee families, including stipends for education and housing. #EconomicEmpowerment

40. Create community-based microloan systems for families to foster entrepreneurship and financial independence. #EconomicEmpowerment

41. Develop hybrid education systems blending traditional schools with technology-driven home-learning environments for better flexibility. #EducationInnovation

42. Advocate for vocational and technical education at the middle and high school levels to prepare students for careers directly after graduation. #EducationInnovation

43. Research and propose innovative family-centered applications of AI to assist with parenting, eldercare, and household management. #TechnologyAndInnovation

44. Encourage tech companies to build family-friendly digital spaces with tools that promote engagement, creativity, and safety. #TechnologyAndInnovation

45. Support government incentives for businesses that offer family-friendly policies, such as remote work and extended leave options. #WorkplaceTransformation

46. Advocate for mandatory sick leave policies that include caregiving responsibilities for family members. #WorkplaceTransformation

47. Develop policies to encourage families to integrate intergenerational living arrangements, providing tax breaks or subsidies for housing that accommodates multi-generational households. #IntergenerationalFamilySupport

48. Create programs to teach financial planning and caregiving skills to younger generations to better prepare them for supporting aging family members. #IntergenerationalFamilySupport

49. Promote the development of "family-friendly cities" with integrated transportation, housing, and social services designed around family needs. #CommunityResilience

50. Encourage partnerships between schools, nonprofits, and local businesses to create mentorship and apprenticeship programs for children and teenagers. #CommunityResilience

51. Develop subsidies for families adopting sustainable practices, such as solar energy use, composting, and urban gardening. #SustainabilityAndEnvironmentalResponsibility

52. Support community farming programs that allow families to participate in food production and sustainability efforts. #SustainabilityAndEnvironmentalResponsibility

53. Advocate for the creation of programs that revive local arts, traditions, and storytelling to strengthen family and community bonds. #SocialAndCulturalRevival

54. Foster cross-cultural family exchange programs that promote under-standing, tolerance, and shared values among diverse communities. #SocialAndCulturalRevival

55. Study and implement family policies from countries with high family stability and happiness indices, such as Sweden, Denmark, and New Zealand. #GlobalBestPractices

56. Encourage bilateral agreements with other nations to promote international research and solutions for family-related challenges. #GlobalBestPractices

57. Support the creation of media and entertainment that pos-itively portrays diverse family structures and values. #FamilyEmpowermentThroughMedia

58. Develop campaigns that promote the importance of family unity and shared values across generations. #FamilyEmpowermentThroughMedia

59. Create family-focused disaster preparedness programs to ensure safety and continuity during natural or man-made crises. #DisasterPreparednessAndResilience

60. Establish networks of support for families displaced by climate change, economic disruptions, or other crises. This menu will have an appeal to different palates. Exhaustive implementation may be altruistic, but it is vital to the success of America and its families.#DisasterPreparednessAndResilience

We have two ways to approach our future:

1. Be like Lot's wife in the biblical story, where she looks back and is turned into a pillar of salt. Continue to look back and make little or no advances.
2. To look forward and envision what can be accomplished short and long-term and begin to make inroads one solution at a time.

Many people in America want things the way they were 50 years ago, but going back is not the answer; going forward with virtuous objectives in mind is the answer.

I see this book making two important contributions:

1. Getting the family on the front burner of this administration and con-vincing it that all the agencies working together for the family is the most

powerful way to build a great country for the future. Support productivity and tremendous value to our world-leading growth.

2. Change the dialogue to a framework of all is not lost, all is not forgotten, and all can be blended. Finding the pathway to reuniting the nation is important. Getting involved, not just as a voter, not as an activist, but as a concerned citizen. Doing away with political rhetoric and focusing on what we all must agree is best for the nation, which is the family.

What we do shows what we are. It is a slap in the face of the American people for our government to say it cares about the family when we have created a family crisis at our southern border. But we are allowing it to happen.

Families (voters) can no longer take a backseat to companies. There needs to be a financial, cultural, economic, and educational incentive to having children, raising them, and having a thriving family. We have gone from an average of 3.7 people in a family in the 60s to 3.14, which is a very sad trend. We can't drastically reduce immigration while population growth shrinks. The United States is 56th in infant mortality deaths. Fifty percent of households in the United States have two parents working. We have become a family-insensitive nation. Only 7% of the US workforce gets paid family leave. Out of 196 countries, the United States is one of two countries not giving family leave. Sweden, for example, offers 480 days of leave at 80% of normal pay plus 18 additional weeks to moms. The Republic of Korea gives 100% for 90 days. Between 1948 and 2001, the percentage of working-age women employed or looking for work nearly doubled from less than 33% to 60%. We need to do much, much better, and this book is drawing a line in the sand to say thus far, no further. Family first or nothing.

Once you have read the book and understood its principles and urgent necessity, it's time to write to Congress and begin the work of changing the future of the American family together.

Scan the code below for a downloadable letter template to create a movement.

EPILOGUE

The American family, once the cornerstone of our nation's identity and strength, stands at a crossroads. Over time, shifting cultural norms, economic pressures, technological advancements, and political neglect have reshaped what it means to be a family. This book has journeyed through the past, present, and potential future of the American family, uncovering both the cracks in its foundation and the possibilities for its revival.

We began by acknowledging the crisis at hand—a landscape where traditional family structures have given way to diverse and evolving forms. This diversity is not a weakness but a strength, yet it requires a reimagined support system to thrive. Families today face unprecedented challenges, from the economic burdens of housing and education to the social isolation exacerbated by digital lives and fractured communities. These are compounded by a lack of robust policies that prioritize the family as the nucleus of societal well-being. The wakeup call has been made. Washington has a golden moment in time to answer the call and design a master plan for the American family that will be hailed as a nation's finest achievement in honoring the pillar of all societies—family.

Through the lens of history, we examined how families have adapted to change, whether during the Industrial Revolution, the rise of the nuclear family, or the digital age. Each era brought opportunities and struggles, but the consistent thread has been the resilience of the family unit when given the right support. However, as we look toward the future, it is clear that survival alone is not enough. We must strive for families to flourish.

Key themes emerged: the need for economic equity and accessible education, the potential and pitfalls of artificial intelligence and social media, the redefinition of parenting roles, and the resurgence of communal values. The pandemic served as both a challenge and a revelation, reminding us of the power of connection, adaptability, and the bonds that define a family—whether chosen or biological.

The solutions are within our grasp. By implementing forward-thinking policies—like paid family leave, universal childcare, equitable housing, and education reform—we can rebuild the scaffolding that allows families to thrive. By embracing technology wisely, fostering intergenerational wisdom, and rekindling the spirit of community, we can restore the American family to its rightful place as the foundation of our national prosperity.

Ultimately, the survival of the family is not just a personal or cultural matter—it is a societal imperative. A thriving family means thriving individuals, communities, and nations. As we close this chapter, let us commit to building a future where every family, in all its forms, is seen, valued, and empowered. For in the family lies the enduring strength of humanity, and in its success lies the promise of a brighter, more compassionate America.

ABOUT THE AUTHOR

Dr. Jerry Cammarata is a distinguished author, educator, and public servant with a career spanning several decades. Known for his contributions to public health, education, and community service, Dr. Cammarata has held various influential positions in government. He has been a vocal advocate for children's health and education, tirelessly working to implement policies that safeguard and promote the well-being of young people. In addition to his public service, Dr. Cammarata is a prolific writer, with works that delve into topics ranging from health policy to personal development. His insightful and impactful publications reflect his commitment to making a positive difference in society, cementing his legacy as a compassionate and dedicated leader.

In 1973, Dr. Jerry Cammarata made history as the first father in the United States to successfully fight for and win a Paternity Leave from the New York City Board of Education, thanks to a new regulation by the Federal Equal Employment Opportunity Commission. This landmark victory paved the way for future changes. Since then, he has continued to innovate as a parent, developing creative methods of childrearing. Dr. Cammarata authored *The Fun Book of Fatherhood*, an autobiographical account of raising his children following his groundbreaking paternity leave. He is also a syndicated columnist ("Father's Diary") and a featured contributor to medical and political journals, as well as newspapers nationwide. In 1980, President Carter appointed Dr. Cammarata to the White House Conference on Families. He was also a syndicated columnist.

In April 2002, Dr. Jerry Cammarata was appointed as the Associate Executive Director of Coney Island Hospital by Mayor Michael Bloomberg's administration. Previously, in July 2000, Mayor Rudolph Giuliani had appointed him as the Commissioner of the Department of Youth and Community Development. During his tenure as Commissioner, Dr. Cammarata significantly impacted youth and community programs, including literacy, citizenship, and after-school initiatives. Before this role,

Mayor Giuliani had also appointed him as Chairman of the Youth Board of the City.

While serving in these capacities, Dr. Cammarata also held a dual role as a Member of the New York City Central Board of Education, serving two terms. As an advocate for children's rights on the Board, he oversaw the education of 1.2 million students, managed 1,100 school buildings, and was responsible for a $12 billion educational budget and a $7 billion capital budget.

Dr. Cammarata was the Assistant Vice President of Community Affairs at Touro University and held several positions at Touro College of Osteopathic Medicine New York, including Chief Operating Officer, Dean of Student Affairs, and Associate Professor. Professionally, Dr. Cammarata is a healthcare management consultant, Speech-Language Pathologist, and Board-Certified Audiologist. He holds degrees from Hofstra University and California Coast University, an Honorary Doctor of Science degree from Mercy College, a Doctor of Humane Letters degree from Dowling College, and the Presidential Medal of Honor from St. John's University. Additionally, he was named Educator of the Year by Phi Delta Kappa of Columbia University.

Dr. Cammarata is currently the Ambassador to the United Nations for the World Safety Organization.

The End.
And hopefully, the beginning of the new American family.

www.ingramcontent.com/pod-product-compliance
Lightning Source LLC
Chambersburg PA
CBHW030526100426
42813CB00001B/166